THE COUNTRYSPORT BOOK OF WILD GAME CUISINE

The Hunter's Table

To

Andy and Nancy
Murphy

Happy Hunting
and

Bon Appetit

Richard Blond

THE COUNTRYSPORT BOOK OF WILD GAME CUISINE

The Hunter's Table

Recipes by
Chef Richard Blondin

Written by
Terry Libby

COUNTRYSPORT PRESS
SELMA, ALABAMA

This edition of *The Hunter's Table* was printed by Jostens Book Manufacturing, State College, Pennsylvania. The book was designed by Saxon Design of Traverse City, Michigan. It is set in Cochin.

First Edition
10 9 8 7 6 5 4 3 2 1

Published by Countrysport Press
Craig Industrial Park, Building 116, Selma, AL 36701

Printed in the United States of America

ISBN 0-924357-80-0 Trade Edition

Library of Congress Cataloging-in-Publication Data

The hunter's table: the countrysport book of wild game cuisine/recipes by Richard Blondin; written by Terry Libby.--1st ed.
    p. cm
Includes index.
ISBN 0-924357-80-0
  1. Cookery (Game) I. Blondin, Richard. II. Title.

TX751 L53 1999
641.6'91--dc21

99-050065

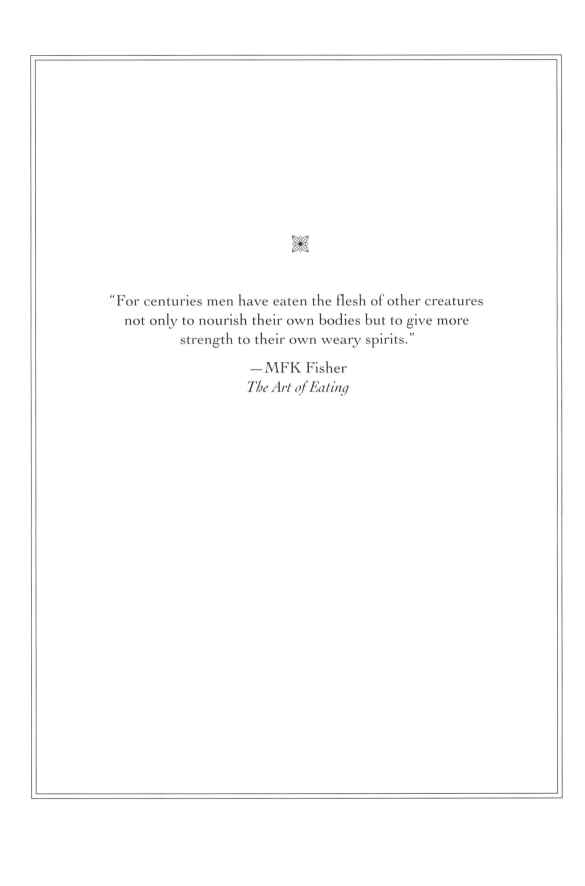

"For centuries men have eaten the flesh of other creatures
not only to nourish their own bodies but to give more
strength to their own weary spirits."

—MFK Fisher
The Art of Eating

Contents

Acknowledgments

I will confess to having been hunting only once in my life. My father, a West Virginian and a hunter and fisherman from boyhood, took me along when I was about nine or ten years old. He let me carry the shotgun, which was as big as I was. Pheasants were our prey. I remember a sudden rustling in the weeds and a huge brown pheasant in lift-off just over my head. My father snatched the gun from me and fired. He missed.

All of us involved in the production of *The Hunter's Table*—Chef Richard Blondin, Countrysport Press, and myself—were brought together by one remarkable person: Doral Chenoweth, a.k.a, "The Grumpy Gourmet," restaurant reviewer for *The Columbus Dispatch* (Columbus, Ohio), for more than 20 years running. Chenoweth's well-cultivated, crusty demeanor strikes both fear and fondness in the hearts of Columbus' restaurateurs. A great food writer and a well-armed critic who takes no prisoners, Chenoweth has kept Columbus engaged in a never-ending but highly beneficial debate about what's worth eating in our town—and what's not. The result: a medium-sized city with a sophisticated assortment of restaurants and a well-informed public.

When Countrysport decided to create its own book of fine game cookery, they asked Chenoweth to recommend a team—a chef and a writer—who could do the job. Without hesitation he suggested that Chef Blondin and I should pair up for the project. We did—and *The Hunter's Table* is the result.

My thanks to Richard Blondin for his patience in working with me over these many months. "A fancy French chef without the 'attitude,' " as Doral Chenoweth describes him, and that's right on the mark. Our work together has been an education for me about the wonders of wild meat, fish and fowl—and a reminder of how much I love all things French.

Paul Poplis's sumptuous photographs pop right off the page. An unforgettable day was spent at his spectacular studio, outfitted with a kitchen any professional chef would envy.

And my thanks also to the very patient and gracious Susan Hunter of Countrysport Press for providing us with this opportunity to share Chef Blondin's talents with game enthusiasts everywhere.

*"Good cooking is ninety percent about experience
and ten percent about the recipe."*

— RICHARD BLONDIN

Chef Richard Blondin

The Hunter's Table presents the recipes of Chef Richard Blondin, Chef de Cuisine at The Refectory in Columbus, Ohio, one of the Midwest's top-rated restaurants, recognized many times over by *The Wine Spectator* for its outstanding and expansive wine cellar.

Richard Blondin's culinary roots are in Lyon, France, where he studied under Pierre Orsi and Paul Bocuse, both chefs of international renown. Blondin was born in nearby Villefrance-sur-Saône, in the heart of the Beaujolais region. Though vineyards and farms dominate the eastern side of the region, the west is mountainous with pine, oak, and chestnut forests full of wild boar, duck, pheasant, hare, and trout. The native cuisine is rural and rustic, and the wild game tradition is strong. For *The Hunter's Table*, Chef Blondin has drawn from the French country style that he knows best from childhood.

Though good varieties of farm-raised game feature prominently on his menu, make no mistake, says Chef Blondin: There is nothing to compare to the flavor of true wild game, fresh from the hunt.

"Territoriality makes the flavor and texture of wild game different from that of all other meats," he says. The diet and movement of animals in the wild produce the qualities of true game prized by Chef Blondin: rich flavor and firm texture. His reputation as an expert game chef has grown, as hunters returned from the field with game birds and venison and searched for a chef who could do justice to the fine meat. Chef Blondin began preparing private game dinners for central Ohio sportsmen. He shares those recipes in *The Hunter's Table*.

The Hunter's Table is intended to be a versatile tool, with many recipes adaptable for experimentation with conventional meats such as beef, lamb, pork, and chicken—with delicious results. (Suggested substitutions are provided for each recipe). Chef Blondin believes that all chefs, including at-home chefs, must follow their instincts first and adhere to the written recipe second. Experience is the best teacher.

"Use your eyes and your palate when you cook," says Blondin, "not the clock." He likes to quote his good friend, Chef Alain Chapel: "There is no such thing as a good recipe. There are only good cooks."

Also included are many traditional accompaniments to game meats: lush potato side dishes including the classic potatoes HUNTER'S POTATOES LYONNAISE *(see page 103)*, fresh wild vegetable preparations, salads, soups, stews, breads, and desserts—even Blondin's family recipe for a special French Hunter's Liqueur, easily fermented at home.

Before You Begin

What is very old is now new again. Game meats began to disappear from the American table around the turn of the century. Our palates changed as mass produced domesticated meat became the cheaper and more desirable option for most households. Indeed, the very word "gamey" took on a decidedly negative connotation. We forgot the methods and finesse of game cookery. Wild game became part of the culinary culture of poor and rustic folk, or the novelty of the very rich who have traditionally dined on exotic game dishes and enjoyed hunting for sport. But the start of a new millennium sees the return of wild game to the top of our list of the most sought-after foods.

Seasonal game menus are featured in fine restaurants everywhere. Chefs are reeducating themselves, reviving and enhancing traditional game preparations. Game farms are flourishing in every region of the U.S. Adventurous diners, both hunters and non-hunters, are willing to sup on fish, meat, and fowl that they've never eaten before.

The return to game meats is a sort of culinary revolution and, in a sense, it's part of the larger cultural phenomenon of getting back to nature, having a greater awareness of what we consume and where it comes from. Much of the farm-raised game available today is organic, chemical-free, and produced in settings that mimic the wild and natural territory of the animals. Add to this the well-established fact that game meats are lower in fat and higher in protein than domesticated meats. The revival of wild game cuisine was inevitable for a generation of consumers concerned with both environmental and health issues—and possessed of an endless appetite for variety.

And so it follows that people want to learn to cook game for themselves.

Buying Game Meats

No doubt about it, the easiest way to locate game meat is via the Internet. Just log onto your favorite search engine and type in "wild game meats." Game farms and ranches have Web pages and on-line catalogues offering everything from rabbit to rattlesnake. Some suppliers provide not only farm-raised game, but can actually ship rare wild game from international markets in Scotland, Africa, Australia, and New Zealand. Do your hunting with a high-caliber credit card because shipping costs can be steep.

Looking for, say, a frenched rack of kangaroo? No problem—contact thriving suppliers such as:

Specialty Game, Inc.
www.specialtygame.com
1-800-998-GAME

D'Artagnan
www.dartagnan.com
1-800-DARTAGNAN

Polarica
www. polarica.com
1-800-426-3872

These and many more fast-growing companies handle fresh game meat, cured and smoked fish and game, sausages, pâtés, grains, wild mushrooms, game condiments, and even exotic produce items.

Farm-raised game is so widely available now that it should come as no surprise that many upscale supermarkets stock it routinely. Look to the organic and health foods industry. All-natural supermarket chains like Wild Oats Markets, Inc. and Whole Foods Markets, Inc. are expanding to cities across the country and often carry game meats like duck, rabbit, boar, and venison plus free-range varieties of beef, lamb, pork, and poultry.

Farmers markets, and organic farming associations can also be good sources for game meats. A good butcher shop should be ready to special-order game meats with a little advance notice, and many chefs may be willing to share information about their game suppliers.

WILD BOAR TERRINE WITH CARAMELIZED FENNEL (pg 18)

GRILLED VENISON TENDERLOINS WRAPPED IN DOUBLE-SMOKED BACON (pg 54),
WITH HUNTER'S POTATOES LYONNAISE (pg 103)

PAN-SEARED SADDLE OF YOUNG HARE IN BEAUJOLAIS NOUVEAU (pg 72), WITH CRISPY CAULIFLOWER CROSTINI (pg 24), AND CREAM CORN RAGOUT

OSTRICH TENDERLOIN AU POIVRE (pg 74)

PAN-SEARED WALLEYE WITH CHARDONNAY CRÉME SAUCE (pg 100),
AND BUTTER-BROWNED POTATO GNOCCI (pg 112)

GUINEA HEN DONE THREE WAYS WITH
ESSENCE OF TRUFFLE (pg 85), RED CURRANT SAUCE FOR GAME (pg 135),
AND COUNTRY FRENCH SCALLOPED POTATOES (pg 106)

LEG OF GUINEA HEN EN CROÛTE (pg 88) WITH
MUSHROOM DUXELLES (pg 126), AND BRAISED RED CABBAGE (pg 128)

WARM APPLE TART WITH ROSEMARY (pg 146)

"Of soup and love, the first is best."

—A bit of French wisdom

Soups, Stews, & Stocks

CREAMY MADEIRA PHEASANT SOUP WITH MUSHROOMS

SERVES 4

1 large pheasant, male, about 3½ pounds

(substitute partridge, wood pigeon, duck)

3 tablespoons unsalted butter

1 small white onion, diced

2 garlic cloves, slivered

2 teaspoons flour

⅓ cup Madeira

6 cups Rich Chicken Stock *(see page 16)*

1 small bouquet garni *(see page 3)*

¼ cup dried green lentils

1 ounce smoked bacon, finely chopped

1 small carrot, diced

½ cup heavy cream

salt and freshly ground black pepper to taste

½ cup fresh mushrooms, sliced

2 tablespoons chopped fresh Italian flatleaf parsley

1   Carefully carve the breast meat from the pheasant. Cover and refrigerate. Cut the remaining carcass into six pieces and coarsely chop the rest of the meat and skin.

2   In a large saucepan, heat 1 tablespoon butter. Pan-sear the carcass and chopped pheasant meat until golden brown on all sides. Add the onion and garlic and cook another 4 minutes. Drain excess fat from the pan.

3   Sprinkle the flour over the meat and carcass and toss well. Deglaze the pan with the Madeira. Add the chicken stock and bouquet garni and simmer, uncovered, 30 minutes. Frequently skim (and discard) fat and foam by floating a broad, shallow spoon over the surface of the simmering stock. Remove the finished stock from the heat and set aside.

4   While the stock simmers, bring a small saucepan of water to a boil. Add the lentils, bacon, and carrot. Boil 10 minutes, or until the lentils are tender. Drain. Puree half the mixture in a blender or food processor. Reserve the other half.

5   Add the lentil puree to the finished stock. Add the cream and salt and pepper to taste. Using a fine wire mesh or chinois, strain the soup into a large saucepan.

6   Melt a second tablespoon of the butter in a small sauté pan and cook the mushrooms over medium-high heat for 3 minutes. Lightly season with salt and pepper. Add the mushrooms, along with the remaining lentil mixture, to the strained soup. Keep the soup very hot.

7   Melt the remaining tablespoon of butter in the pan in which the mushrooms were sautéed. Season the pheasant breasts with salt and pepper and sear them in the butter for about 2 minutes per side, to medium-rare. Remove from the pan at once.

8   To serve, carve each breast crosswise into 8 thin slices. Place four slices in each soup bowl and pour in the hot soup. Garnish with chopped parsley and an added splash of Madeira.

A NOTE ON THE
CLASSIC BOUQUET GARNI…

As you'll see, Chef Blondin makes frequent use of the classic French bouquet garni—a small bundle of fresh herbs tied with twine. Parsley, bay leaves, and thyme are the standard ingredients, but tarragon, chives, and other herbs can be used as well. The point of the bouquet garni is to infuse the dish with flavor. It's placed in the pot at the early stages of preparation and removed before the dish is served, leaving the broth clear and uncluttered. It is more the Italian or American style of cooking to chop the herbs before adding them to the pot and to leave them in the finished dish. There is no hard and fast rule here—chop your herbs if you prefer!—or go French and make yourself a tidy bouquet garni.

Hearty Duck Hunter's Sausage and Potato Soup

Serves 8

A rich, brothy soup to serve with fresh-baked
Hunter's Foccacia (see page 133) and a good bottle of Cabernet.

8 pounds duck carcasses
(substitute wild goose or chicken)
water to cover, 3 to 4 quarts
1 small Savoy cabbage
3 large carrots, peeled and chopped
2 turnips, peeled and chopped
1 pound duck sausage, or other smoked sausage
3 tablespoons unsalted butter
2 medium white onions, diced
4 medium potatoes (about 1½ pounds), peeled and diced
3 tablespoons chopped, fresh Italian flatleaf parsley

1   Place the duck carcasses in a deep stockpot and cover with water. Season lightly with salt and pepper, bring to a boil and simmer, covered, for one hour. To achieve a clear stock, check the pot frequently and skim off the excess fat and solids that rise to the surface with a wide, shallow spoon.

2   Peel the stocky outer leaves from the cabbage and coarsely chop the heart. Add the chopped cabbage, carrots, and turnips and to the stock, return to a boil and simmer, covered, an additional 30 minutes. Remove the pan from the heat, season to taste with salt and pepper and set aside to cool slightly. Strain the stock, discarding the carcasses and vegetables. (Yield: 2 quarts stock.)

3   In a hot broiler, cook the sausages until well-browned, then cut into large slices.

4   Melt the butter in a large soup pot. Add the onions and potatoes and cook over medium heat until the onions are translucent, about 5 minutes. Add the reserved stock to the pot and return to a boil. Simmer, uncovered, for 10 minutes, then add the sliced sausages. Serve very hot, garnished with chopped parsley.

Peasant Soup of Smoked Bacon Wild Boar, and Vegetables

Serves 4 to 6

4 quarts water

14 ounces lean, smoked bacon

1 to 2½-pound wild boar butt

(substitute pork butt or fresh ham)

3 carrots, whole, peeled

1 small celery root, peeled

1 small head green cabbage, coarsely chopped

6 medium-sized Yukon Gold potatoes, whole, peeled

3 large leeks, trimmed, washed, and cut in half lengthwise

salt and freshly ground pepper

8 to 10 thick slices of French bread, well-buttered and toasted

1   Put the water, bacon, and boar butt into a deep 5 or 6 quart stockpot. Bring to boil, cover, and reduce heat to a simmer. Cook for 1½ hours or until fork-tender.

2   Uncover the soup and add the whole carrots and the whole celery root. [Note: the vegetables in this soup are chopped at the end of the cooking process to retain flavor and texture.] Cover and cook an additional 15 minutes, then add the cabbage, the whole potatoes, and the leeks. Continue to cook for 20 minutes longer, or until the vegetables are tender.

3   Have ready a large soup terrine, or individual serving bowls. Remove the bacon and wild boar butt from the pot and set aside until cool enough to dice the meat into large chunks. Remove the vegetables from the stock and set aside. Taste the stock and season with additional salt and pepper if needed. Degrease the soup stock if necessary by skimming off the excess fat with a wide, shallow spoon, or a degreasing ladle.

4   To serve, cut the whole vegetables in half and place them in the soup terrine, or distribute them among the serving bowls. Add the meat and bacon chunks and pour in the hot soup stock. Garnish each bowl with a crisp, buttery slice of bread.

CREAM OF MOREL SOUP

SERVES 4

*The dried morels must be soaked a day in advance
to prepare this special cream, and Madeira-laced soup.*

1 cup dried morel mushrooms
1 tablespoon unsalted butter
2 medium shallots, minced
1 cup fresh wild or domestic mushrooms, thinly sliced
1 tablespoon flour
6 cups rich chicken or duck stock *(see page 16)*
1 bouquet garni *(see page 3)*
1 tablespoon olive oil
1 cup Madeira
2 cups heavy cream
salt and freshly ground pepper to taste

1   Soak the morels, undisturbed, in 4 cups of water for 24 hours. As the morels expand, they will shed some of their soil. The morels will float to the surface and the debris will sink to the bottom of the bowl. Lift the morels from the bowl with a slotted spoon. Rinse them again under running water to make sure they are very clean. Drain and set aside.

2   Heat the butter in a large, heavy saucepan over medium heat. Add half the minced shallots and all the sliced fresh mushrooms. Sauté until the mushrooms are golden brown and their liquid has evaporated. Sprinkle the flour over the mushrooms and stir to blend.

3   In a separate pan, bring the stock to a boil. Slowly pour the stock over the mushrooms, stirring constantly. Add the bouquet garni, lower heat to a simmer and cook, covered, for 30 minutes.

4   Heat the olive oil in a small skillet and add the remaining minced shallots. Cook until the shallots are translucent, 3 to 5 minutes. Add the reserved morels and toss gently to brown them. Deglaze the pan with the Madeira and remove from heat.

5   Strain the mushroom and stock mixture and remove the bouquet garni. Puree the solids until very smooth in a blender or food processor, adding stock as needed. At this stage the puree can be strained through a fine wire mesh or chinois to ensure a velvet consistency.

6   Heat the cream in a small saucepan. Return the puree and stock to the soup pot, along with the Madeira and morels. Heat over medium flame and whisk in the warm cream. Bring to a gentle simmer and cook an additional 15 minutes or until thickened. Season to taste with salt and pepper.

"Americans don't trust chefs. In France they respect the art of the profession. No one would dare to ask the chef to alter his recipe to suit their taste. In America they do it all the time! Never, never do this in France."

—R. BLONDIN

Bistro Onion Soup au Gratin
with Champagne and Sherry

Serves 6

Egg yolks and Champagne give this version of
classic French onion soup a velvety texture.

6 tablespoons unsalted butter
6 medium yellow onions, peeled and thinly sliced (about 6 cups)
¾ cup sherry
2 quarts chicken, or duck stock *(see page 16)*
1 bouquet garni *(see page 3)*
salt and freshly ground pepper to taste
½ cup dry Champagne
2 egg yolks
12 ¼-inch-thick slices French baguette, buttered and toasted
12 slices Gruyère cheese
2 tablespoons grated Parmesan

1 Melt the butter in a heavy Dutch oven or soup pot over medium heat. Add the
   onions and cook, stirring often, until caramelized and dark brown in color,
   about 30 to 40 minutes.

2 When the onions are brown, add the sherry and stir to deglaze the pan.
   Cook 5 minutes.

3 Add the stock and bouquet garni and simmer, uncovered, for 30 minutes more.
   Remove from heat and season with salt and pepper to taste. Soup can be made
   ahead up to this point, then reheated just prior to serving.

4 Preheat the broiler. Place 6 broilerproof soup crocks on a sturdy baking sheet.

5 Whisk the Champagne together with the egg yolks until light and foamy.
   Put 1½ tablespoons of this mixture in each crock, then pour in the hot onion soup.
   Place two slices of toasted baguette on each crock, topped with two slices of
   Gruyère. Dust each crock with grated Parmesan.

6 Transfer the crocks to the oven and broil until the cheese is bubbly and golden
   brown, about 5 to 7 minutes. Serve immediately.

Butternut Squash Soup
with Crisp Potatoes

SERVES 6 TO 8

½ cup chopped leeks (about 1 medium-sized leek, trimmed)

1 butternut squash, about 1½ pounds

¼ cup chopped onion

2 tablespoons minced celery

2 tablespoons unsalted butter

3 cups whole milk

2 tablespoons canola oil

2 cups peeled and finely diced potatoes (⅓-inch cubes)

salt and freshly ground black pepper to taste

2 tablespoons fresh chopped chives

1 To chop the leek, trim at both ends leaving about 2 to 3 inches of light green stalk. Slice lengthwise and pull the layers apart and rinse thoroughly. Chop into ½-inch-thick slices, rinse again, and drain.

2 Peel the squash, then cut in half and remove the seeds by scraping with a soup spoon. Cut the squash into ½-inch cubes.

3 Heat the butter in a large saucepan. Sauté the leeks, onion, and celery over medium heat for about 8 minutes. Add the squash and sauté another 4 minutes. Add the milk and bring to a simmer. Cook, uncovered, for 30 minutes.

4 Let the mixture cool slightly, then puree the soup in 2 or 3 batches in a blender or food processor until very smooth. Return to the saucepan and keep warm.

5 Heat the oil in a sauté pan. Add the potatoes and sauté over high heat until crispy brown. Drain on paper towels.

6 To preserve their crispy texture, add the potatoes to the soup bowl just prior to serving. Garnish each bowl with fresh chives.

"Burgundy makes you think of silly things; Bordeaux makes you talk about them, and Champagne makes you do them."

— BRILLAT-SAVARIN

GROUPER SOUP

SERVES 4

Something like a brothy bouillabaisse, the key to this soup
is the doublyrich base of fish stock laced with saffron and Pernod.
It is a favorite with guests at The Refectory, where
Chef Blondin oversees the preparation of every pot!

4 tablespoons olive oil

2 large carrots, diced

3 pounds grouper bones

(substitute monkfish or striped bass bones)

1 large white onion, chopped

5 cloves fresh garlic, minced

2 stalks celery, diced

8 ripe plum tomatoes, diced

6 cups FISH STOCK *(see page 15)*

8 ounces grouper fillet, skin removed

6 tablespoons butter, divided (keep 2 tablespoons chilled in the refrigerator)

4 tablespoons flour

1 bouquet garni *(see page 3)*

pinch of saffron, about ¼ teaspoon

2 tablespoons Pernod (available at most liquor stores)

salt and freshly ground white and black pepper to taste

1   To prepare the soup base, heat the olive oil over high heat in a heavy stock pot. Add the carrots and sauté for 5 minutes. Add the fish bones, onion, garlic, and celery. Cook, stirring constantly, until a heavy browned glaze forms on the bottom of the pan, about 15 minutes. Do not burn the mixture.

2   Stir in the diced tomatoes, scraping the bottom of the pan to deglaze. Pour in the fish stock and bring to a boil. Remove the pan from the heat and set aside until cool enough to handle.

3   Strain the soup through a fine wire mesh or chinois. Set aside.

4   Cut the grouper fillet into bite-sized chunks and season with salt and white pepper.

5 Melt the butter (4 tablespoons) in a heavy saucepan over medium heat. Add the grouper and sauté until light brown. Add the flour and stir.

6 Slowly pour the reserved soup into the pan, stirring gently to avoid breaking up the fish chunks. Add the bouquet garni, saffron, and Pernod. Bring to a simmer and cook over low heat, partially covered, for 30 minutes.

7 To finish, remove the bouquet garni, whisk in the 2 tablespoons of chilled butter, and season to taste with salt and fresh black pepper.

A WORD ABOUT GARLIC...

In Chef Blondin's kitchen, much time is spent peeling fresh garlic and removing the green "germ" from the center of each clove, a step typical in French cooking. It is the germ that has a bitter aftertaste and is hard to digest. The whole crew is required to take a turn at the tedious task of garlic trimming—even the dishwashers.

"If you love garlic, you can add it to virtually any recipe," says Chef Blondin. "All Mediterranean cooking uses plenty of garlic. You'll need a good, sharp Syrah wine with a garlicky dish. The Syrah grape comes from the Middle East—Iran and Iraq—where they use lots of garlic. Yes, garlic is always welcome."

Cabernet-Drenched Wild Elk Stew with Pearl Onions

Serves 8

¼ cup fine quality olive oil

10 ounces smoked bacon, cut into ½ dice

30 to 40 fresh, peeled pearl onions *(substitute small shallots)*

6 ounces of elk meat, leg or shoulder, cut into 1-inch cubes

(substitute black bear, moose, boar, beef, or lamb)

6 medium carrots, diced

3 stalks celery, diced

3 tablespoons all-purpose flour

6 cloves garlic, minced

2 bay leaves

large pinch dried thyme

1½ tablespoons tomato paste

4-5 cups good-quality Cabernet Sauvignon

3 tablespoons unsalted butter

12 ounces fresh mushrooms, sliced

¼ chopped fresh Italian flatleaf parsley

1   To peel the pearl onions, cut a tiny X at the base of each one, then drop them into rapidly boiling water for one minute. Drain the onions quickly and, when cool enough to handle, peel away the thin outer layer.

2   Heat the oil in a heavy skillet. Add the diced bacon and the onions *(or shallots)* and cook over medium heat until golden brown, 7 to 10 minutes. With a slotted spoon, remove the bacon and onions from the skillet and set aside.

3   Increase the heat to high and add the cubed elk meat to the pan. Season with salt and pepper, and sauté the meat until it is well browned on all sides, about 5 minutes.

4   Add the carrots and celery and continue to cook, covered, for 10 minutes.

5   Sprinkle the flour evenly over the meat and vegetables and mix well.

6 Add the garlic, bay leaves, thyme, tomato paste, and then return the reserved bacon and onion mixture to the pan. Stir well and add 4 cups of the wine. If the wine does not cover the elk meat, add up to one additional cup to cover.

7 Cover and cook over low heat for two hours.

8 When you are ready to serve the stew, melt the butter in another skillet and sauté the sliced mushrooms over medium heat for 2 to 3 minutes. Season with additional salt and pepper to taste.

9 To serve, pour the stew into a decorative soup terrine or casserole, top with the sautéed mushrooms, and garnish with the chopped parsley. Serve over pasta, rice, or potatoes.

CHEF BLONDIN'S RICH GAME STOCK

MAKES 1 QUART

1 cup plus 2 tablespoons canola oil

4 pounds bones from wild game, cut into pieces about 3 inches long

2 pounds game bird carcasses

1 large leek, minced

3 carrots, minced

2 stalks celery, minced

5 shallots, minced

2 medium onions, quartered

3 ounces tomato paste

4 ounces brandy

750ml bottle of good quality red wine

8 cups CHICKEN STOCK (*see page 16, or use canned*)

1   Preheat the oven to 400° F. Pour one cup of the canola oil into a shallow roasting pan large enough to hold all the bones and carcasses. Toss the 3-inch bones in the oil to coat them evenly. Brown them in the oven for 20 minutes.

2   Remove the pan from the oven, add the game bird carcasses, and toss again to coat with oil. Return the pan to the oven and roast for an additional 20 minutes.

3   In a skillet, heat 2 tablespoons canola oil. Add the leek, carrots, celery, shallots, and onions. Sauté the vegetables over medium heat until richly browned, about 20 minutes. Stir in the tomato paste and brandy.

4   When the bones are done, remove them from the roasting pan and place them in a large stockpot. Deglaze the hot roasting pan with the wine, combining it with any pan drippings and scraping the bottom to dislodge flavorful brown bits. Add this mixture to the stockpot.

5   Add the sautéed vegetable mixture and the chicken stock to the wine and the bones. Bring to a boil, reduce the heat and simmer for 4 hours. Frequently skim (and discard) fat and foam by floating a broad, shallow spoon over the surface of the stock.

6   Strain the stock through a fine wire mesh strainer into a bowl, and refrigerate. Additional fat will rise to the surface once the stock is cold, and can be scraped away. When you are ready to use the stock, reheat and continue to reduce it over high heat until slightly thickened and the flavor is rich. Season the finished stock with salt and pepper to taste.

FISH STOCK

MAKES 2 QUARTS

2½ pounds fish trimmings: bones, skin and tails
1 leek, sliced, white part only
1 white onion, coarsely chopped
2 stalks celery, sliced
5-6 sprigs fresh Italian flatleaf parsley
2 cups dry white wine
cold water
1 bay leaf

1   Thoroughly rinse the fish trimmings in cold running water. Place the leek, onion, celery, and parsley in a 3-quart stock pot. Place the fish trimmings over the vegetables and add the wine.

2   Add water to barely cover the fish. Bring to simmer over medium heat and add the bay leaf.

3   Simmer, partially covered, for 45 minutes, stirring occasionally. Remove from heat and let the stock cool completely. Strain through cheesecloth or a very fine wire mesh.

MAKING A FINE GAME STOCK

What are the tricks to making a rich and flavorful stock? First, says Chef Blondin, comes patience. A stock must be simmered for a very long time, never boiled, and the foam and fat must be skimmed from the surface many, many times during this process. A good stock is pricey to make. It requires a great deal of good, meaty carcass bones, roasted just until they are caramelized and a nice, deep brown color. Burnt bones will make for a bitter stock.

"If you have a bad stock," says Chef Blondin, "you will never have a good sauce."

Rich Stock of Chicken, Rabbit, or Duck

Makes 2 quarts (8 cups)

5 pounds fresh chicken, rabbit, or duck bones

1 gallon water

1 large carrot, peeled and diced

2 medium white onions, diced (about 1½ cups)

3 bay leaves

3 stalks celery, diced

1 small leek, chopped

2 large sprigs fresh parsley

1 large branch fresh thyme

1 cup fresh mushrooms, chopped

1   Place the chicken, rabbit, or duck bones in a large stock pot. Include neck bones if available. Add the water and place over high heat. Bring to a boil, then reduce to a simmer.

2   Add all the rest of the ingredients, stir, and continue to simmer for 1½ hours. To achieve a clear consistency, skim the surface of the stock every 10 minutes with a shallow spoon to remove excess foam and fat.

3   Remove the pot from the heat and let the stock cool slightly. Strain it through a very fine wire mesh sieve or a layer of cheesecloth. Store the stock, well covered, in the refrigerator for up to 3 days. Stock can be kept in the freezer for up to 6 months.

Note: For cubes of ready-made bouillon, pour stock into an ice cube tray and freeze, then release the cubes into a zip-lock plastic bag to store in the freezer.

*"Love and hunger share the same purpose.
Life must never cease—life must be sustained and must create."*
—TURGENEV

Wild Appetizers

Wild Boar Terrine
with Caramelized Fennel

Preparing a classic terrine may seem like a daunting task, but your investment of some extra time and patience will be richly rewarded. Encasing the terrine in thin slices of pork fatback, also called barding fat, will seal juices and flavors into the finished product as it bakes, but the fatback can be omitted if the mixture is baked in a heavy loaf pan. This terrine makes an impressive first course or centerpiece for a cocktail party buffet. Crusty French bread and tart little pickles known as cornichons are traditional accompaniments.

¼ cup brandy

¼ cup port

¼ cup dry (white) vermouth

1 teaspoon fresh, chopped sage

6 whole juniper berries

18 ounces wild boar shoulder

1 cup fresh fennel, cut into ⅓-inch-thick slices

¼ cup canola oil

1 ounce Pernod

¼ cup unsalted butter

3 ounces fresh chicken livers

¼ cup finely minced shallots

9 ounces wild boar loin

(Substitute hare, elk, wild sheep, or pork)

3 ounces pork liver

4 ounces lightly smoked bacon

¼ cup finely diced carrots

2 whole eggs, lightly beaten

1½ pounds pork fatback or "barding fat," sliced into very thin strips or sheets

¼ cup whole, cooked chestnuts (fresh or canned chestnuts)

salt and freshly ground black pepper to taste

1   In a medium glass mixing bowl, blend together the brandy, port, vermouth, sage, and juniper berries. Cut the boar shoulder into 1-inch cubes and toss with this

marinade. Cover and refrigerate for 3 hours.

2   In a medium saucepan, bring two cups of water to a boil. Add the sliced fennel along with a pinch of salt and boil for about 20 minutes, until the fennel is very tender. Drain thoroughly in a colander.

3   Heat the canola oil in a skillet over medium-high heat. Add the cooked fennel and sauté until it is caramelized, about 8 minutes. Deglaze the pan with the Pernod; remove from heat.

4   In another skillet, melt the butter. Add the chicken livers and shallots and sauté over high heat for 2 minutes, leaving the chicken livers with pink centers to retain their juices. Quickly remove the pan from the heat and place the chicken livers and all pan drippings together into a small bowl and set aside.

5   Reserving the liquid, strain the boar shoulder cubes, sage, and juniper berries from the marinade; coarsely grind these 3 ingredients together. Then grind together the boar loin, pork liver and the bacon (these can be ground into the same bowl as the shoulder meat.)

6   Drain the cooked chicken livers and set aside, reserving the shallots and pan drippings. In a large mixing bowl, combine the pan drippings, shallots, and reserved marinade with all the ground meat, carrots, caramelized fennel, and eggs. Add salt and pepper to taste.

7   Preheat the oven to 350°F. Begin heating a saucepan of water to a simmer.

8   Prepare a 2½-quart terrine or loaf pan by lining it with overlapping slices of the pork fatback. Place the slices crosswise along the bottom and sides of the pan, leaving enough excess overhang to cover the top of the filling. NOTE: If you are omitting the fatback, thoroughly butter the inside of the terrine or loaf pan before adding the meat mixture.

9   Fill the terrine with half the ground meat mixture. Wrap each chicken liver in a very thin wrapper of fatback (optional). Alternate chicken livers and whole chestnuts, spacing them evenly in a neat row down the center of the pan and pressing lightly into the meat mixture. Add the remaining meat mixture and smooth the top of the terrine with a spatula.

10 Fold the overhanging slices of fatback on top to seal. Tightly cover the pan with a lid or aluminum foil. Place another baking pan (large enough to hold the terrine) on the center oven rack. Place the terrine in the pan and fill the pan with about one inch of simmering water to make a bain-marie (water bath).

11 Bake for 1 hour and 10 minutes. Remove the cover and arrange weights on top of the terrine while it cools completely. (Use cans or any other weighty object, but no more than 2 pounds. Pressing the terrine as it cools will give it the proper texture and density.) Chill at least two hours, then slice and serve.

SMOKED
SALMON SPREAD

MAKES ABOUT 1½ TO 2 CUPS SPREAD

A satisfying snack after a long day's hunt, or an elegant addition to a party buffet.
Use this spread on slices of hot French bread straight from the oven.

½ cup white wine
4 tablespoons shallots, thinly sliced
4 ounces fresh salmon, bones and skin removed
(substitute fresh Arctic char or trout, or a combination)
6 ounces smoked salmon, cut into very fine strips
1 tablespoon chopped fresh chives
1 tablespoon chopped fresh Italian flatleaf parsley
¾ cup unsalted butter, room temperature
salt and freshly ground pepper to taste

1   Add the wine to a saucepan and bring to a boil. Add the shallots and the fresh salmon. Poach for 2 minutes, then remove the pan from the heat, cover, and set aside for 5 minutes more.

2   Drain the poached salmon and the shallots from the wine and set aside to cool completely. Discard the wine.

3   In a mixing bowl, combine the smoked salmon, the poached salmon with the shallots, the chives, parsley, and soft butter. Fold the ingredients together until the mixture is smooth and spreadable. Season to taste with salt and pepper and place in a decorative mold or airtight container. Serve chilled.

CRISP VENISON FRITTERS

MAKES 4 SERVINGS, OR 16 FRITTERS

1 pound venison shoulder

(substitute wild boar or pork)

2 tablespoons unsalted butter

2 tablespoons walnut oil

½ cup fresh button mushrooms, minced

¼ cup flour, plus additional for dredging fritters

salt and freshly ground black pepper to taste

freshly grated nutmeg, to taste

¾ cup heavy cream

¼ cup CHICKEN STOCK *(see page 16, or use canned, unsalted)*

2 whole eggs, beaten

2 cups fine, unseasoned bread crumbs

4 cups pure vegetable oil for deep frying

¼ cup minced fresh Italian flatleaf parsley, plus 2 tablespoons for garnish

1   Slice the venison into fine julienne strips. Melt 1 tablespoon of the butter in a skillet. Add the walnut oil. When the pan is hot, quickly sauté the venison until just lightly browned, then remove the meat from the skillet and set aside.

2   Add the remaining tablespoon of butter to the skillet. When hot, add the mushrooms and sauté for about 5 minutes, or until the liquid has evaporated. Sprinkle the ¼ cup flour over the mushroom mixture, stirring constantly to blend. Season to taste with salt, pepper, and nutmeg.

3   Slowly stir in the chicken stock and cream, stirring constantly until the sauce thickens. [1 cup liquid should make a thick sauce.]Return the venison to the pan and mix it thoroughly with the sauce. Let cool completely.

4   When completely cooled, divide the mixture into about 16 rounded tablespoons and shape into small balls. Dredge the balls in flour, dip into the beaten egg mixture, then roll in bread crumbs to coat evenly.

5   Place the balls on a baking sheet lined with waxed or parchment paper. Refrigerate for at least one hour.

6   In a deep, heavy saucepan, heat the oil to 360°F. Carefully drop in the fritters and fry until golden brown, about 3 minutes. Quickly drain on paper towels and serve very hot, garnished with fresh chopped parsley.

BRANDIED DUCK LIVER PÂTÉ

SERVES 4

2 tablespoons RENDERED DUCK FAT *(see page 140)*
1 small onion, sliced
½ pound fresh duck livers
(substitute goose or chicken liver)
2 tablespoons brandy
¼ cup unsalted butter, soft
salt and freshly ground black pepper to taste
1 tablespoon chopped fresh Italian flatleaf parsley
2 tablespoons dried prunes, cut into very fine strips

1   Heat the duck fat in a heavy skillet over medium-high heat. Sauté the onion and livers together for 10 minutes. Deglaze the pan with the brandy, then flame it by tilting the pan to one side and igniting the pan juices with a long match or flambé tool. Allow the brandy to burn away as you swirl the pan over the heat.

2   Scrape the contents of the skillet into a bowl and set aside to cool to room temperature.

3   In a food processor combine the livers, onion, and pan drippings with the soft butter and salt and pepper to taste. For a very smooth-textured pâté, force the mixture through a fine wire mesh sieve or chinois. Mix in the chopped parsley and prune strips.

4   Put the pâté in a small serving bowl or decorative terrine just large enough to hold all the mixture. Smooth and level the surface. Cover tightly with plastic wrap and chill for at least 3 hours before serving.

5   To serve, prepare a mixed green salad with mustard vinaigrette and serve a portion of pâté in the center of each salad plate along with a crusty bread or toasted croutons.

TART OF WILD LEEKS IN CUSTARD

SERVES 4 AS A MAIN COURSE, 6 TO 8 AS AN APPETIZER

Wild leeks, also called ramps, appear in early spring and can sometimes be found
at farmers markets. If you can find them, by all means use them to make this tart.
If not, standard leeks will do nicely.

1 sheet prepared puff pastry (ready-made is fine)
1½ cups sliced fresh ramps, roots and stalky ends trimmed,
or 3 large cultivated leeks, trimmed, white parts only
3 tablespoons unsalted butter
1 cup heavy cream
1 cup whole milk
4 whole eggs
½ teaspoon salt
freshly ground pepper to taste
pinch of grated nutmeg
¼ cup fine dry bread crumbs

1   Preheat the oven to 350°F. Roll out the pastry to ⅛-inch thickness and line a 9-inch pie or tart pan. When the oven is hot, partially bake the pastry shell for 7 minutes, then remove from the oven and set aside to cool.

2   Wash the leeks(ramps) thoroughly, separating the layers under running water, and drain. Cut the leeks(ramps) into thin slices.

3   Bring a large saucepan of water to a boil and blanch the sliced leeks(ramps) for 2 minutes. Drain and rinse with cold water.

4   Melt the butter in a heavy skillet and cook the leeks(ramps) until they are very soft, about 15 minutes.

5   In a mixing bowl, beat together the cream, milk, and eggs. Add salt, pepper, and nutmeg.

6   Spread the cooked leeks in an even layer in the pastry shell, place on a rack in the oven, then pour in the egg mixture. Top with the bread crumbs and bake for 30 minutes, or until a knife tip inserted in the center of the custard comes out clean.

7   Allow the tart to cool slightly, then cut into wedges and serve garnished with mixed salad greens dressed with vinaigrette.

CRISPY
CAULIFLOWER CROSTINI

MAKES 4 APPETIZERS

*A hot, toasted hors d'oeuvre to enjoy after the hunt
and with a well-deserved cocktail.*

½ medium head of cauliflower, broken into florets
½ cup CLASSIC BÉCHAMEL SAUCE *(see page 141)*
2 tablespoons extra virgin olive oil
½ cup unsalted butter
4 slices of firm white bread, crusts trimmed
1 egg white, stiffly beaten
⅓ cup grated imported Gruyere cheese
½ cup fine dry bread crumbs
salt and freshly ground white pepper to taste
pinch of grated nutmeg

1   Boil or steam the cauliflower until very tender, about 10 minutes. Drain well.

2   Puree the cauliflower in the bowl of a food processor until smooth. Transfer to a small mixing bowl and blend in the Béchamel sauce. Season with salt and pepper to taste.

3   Preheat the oven to 425°F. Heat the oil and 6 tablespoons of the butter in a heavy skillet and add the bread slices. Cook the slices, turning frequently, until they are golden brown on both sides. Place them on a nonstick cookie sheet.

4   Fold the beaten egg white into the cauliflower mixture. Spread a generous spoonful of the mixture on each bread slice. Top with the grated cheese and the bread crumbs, then dot with the remaining 2 tablespoons of butter. Bake for about 3 to 5 minutes, until puffy and golden. Serve hot from the oven.

Great Lakes Smelt Pickled in Champagne Vinegar

2 pounds fresh Great Lakes smelt
(substitute any small lake fish)
leaves from 1 head fresh fennel
½ cup Champagne vinegar *(or white wine vinegar)*
1 cup water
6 white peppercorns
pinch of ground cloves
pinch of grated nutmeg
1 bay leaf
2 teaspoons salt
2 teaspoons sugar

1   Clean and gut the smelt, trimming the heads and backbones. Dry them in a kitchen towel.

2   Arrange the smelt in a single layer in a shallow glass pan, folding a sprig of fresh fennel inside each fish.

3   In a saucepan, combine the remaining ingredients. Stir and bring to a boil. Simmer, uncovered, for 5 minutes. Pour the hot marinade over the fish. Cover and refrigerate for 24 hours to allow the flavors to develop.

4   To serve, transfer the smelt to a serving platter. Serve with warm Hunter's Focaccia (page 133) and Country Herb and Roquefort Butter (see page 132).

Pan-Seared Quail
in Hazelnut Vinaigrette

Makes 4 first-course servings

14 ounces of fresh haricots verts (tiny French green beans)
(substitute very young, freshly picked conventional green beans)
2 quarts water
2 tablespoons salt
1 tablespoon canola oil
2 tablespoons unsalted butter
2 large quail, cleaned, whole
(substitute wild ouzel, rail, or any very small game bird)
3 tablespoons red wine vinegar
2 teaspoons Dijon mustard
2 tablespoons heavy cream
6 tablespoons hazelnut oil
salt and freshly ground black pepper to taste

1   Trim the haricots verts or green beans.

2   In a large saucepan or stock pot, bring the water to a full boil and add the salt. Fill a large bowl with very cold water and set aside. Add the beans to the boiling pot and cook for about 3½ minutes *(5 minutes for green beans)*, until the beans are tender-crisp. Drain the beans as soon as they are done and plunge them into the cold water to retain their crispness and bright color. Drain the beans again and set aside.

3   Preheat the oven to 400°F. In an ovenproof skillet or roasting pan, heat the oil and butter. Sear the quail over medium-high heat, turning constantly to brown on all sides, about 3 minutes. Immediately transfer the pan to the preheated oven and roast for 7 minutes. Do not overcook the birds—the meat should be tender and slightly pink when done.

4   Remove the pan from the oven. Transfer the birds to a carving platter and cover with foil.

5   Drain any excess fat from the pan and deglaze with the vinegar over medium heat. Whisk in the mustard and cream. Slowly drizzle in the hazelnut oil, whisking constantly to make a smooth emulsion. Season to taste with salt and pepper.

6   Carve the breast and leg meat from the birds; slice. Have ready 4 warm appetizer plates.

7   Add the beans to the sauce and toss until just heated through. On each plate, spoon the warm sauce and beans in the center. Arrange the quail slices on top. Serve immediately.

It is customary in Europe to close one's place of business and take a lengthy vacation or break during the month of August. Chef Paul Bocuse closed his Lyon restaurant each year and would invite an underling to act as caretaker of his home and business.

For a few seasons Richard Blondin, then an apprentice chef, volunteered for the job. Sometimes it involved cooking simple meals for Bocuse, who often requested just a simple plate of freshly picked haricots verts—baby green beans. Blondin would simmer the beans in unsalted water until they were tender, but still vivid green in color, then toss them with a bit of butter and a little salt and pepper. Nothing pleased Bocuse so much.

Savory Quail Pie with White Corn and Swiss Cheese

Serves 4 as an appetizer

For the Pastry:

2 cups all-purpose flour

2 whole eggs

¾ cup chilled Rendered Duck Fat *(see page 140, or substitute unsalted butter)*

2 tablespoons milk

1 teaspoon salt

For the Filling:

4 tablespoons unsalted butter

1 small white onion, diced

¾ cup fresh white corn kernels

2½ cups heavy cream

2 tablespoons olive oil

4 whole quail, 8-10 ounces each

(substitute any fresh or left over game poultry)

4 whole eggs

½ cup grated Swiss cheese, such as Gruyère or Emmenthaler

salt and freshly ground pepper to taste

pinch of ground nutmeg

1   Pastry: Put the flour in a large mixing bowl. Add 2 eggs, the duck fat *(or butter)*, milk, and salt, and mix with a paddle or spatula until smooth. Form the dough into a ball, cover tightly with plastic wrap, and refrigerate while the filling is prepared.

2   Filling: Melt 2 tablespoons of the butter in a skillet over medium heat. Add the onion and corn kernels and cook together for 3 minutes. Add ½ cup of the cream and simmer over low heat for 5 minutes more. Remove the pan from the heat and set aside.

3   In another skillet large enough to hold the quail, heat the olive oil and remaining 2 tablespoons of butter over medium heat. Add the quail and cook gently, basting with pan juices, until golden on all sides, about 7 minutes.

4   Remove the pan from the heat and set aside until the quail are cool enough to handle. Remove the breast and leg meat, discarding skin and bones. Cut the meat into long strips.

5   Preheat the oven to 350°F. Turn the dough out onto a lightly floured surface and roll to ⅛-inch thickness. Butter and flour an 8-inch pie pan and line it with the prepared pastry. Arrange the meat slices in the pie, then cover with the corn mixture.

6   Sprinkle the grated cheese evenly over the pie. Beat together the 4 eggs and remaining 2 cups heavy cream. Season with salt, pepper, and nutmeg. Pour the egg and cream mixture slowly over the pie to fill the crust.

7   Bake for 35 minutes, or until a knife inserted in the center of the custard comes out clean. Cool slightly, then slice and serve.

MACHON

The traditional snack of Lyon is called "the mâchon." This is a bit comparable to the Spanish tradition of enjoying tappas with friends at the end of the work day in the late afternoon. Some Lyonnaise restaurants have made the mâchon their specialty. There is even a society—the "Francs-Machon"—for the preservation of the mâchon tradition.

Bottles of Beaujolais accompany things as sausages, salads, cold sliced rabbit and tripe, and fluffy omelettes with potatoes and sorrel, all served with garlicky dressings made with butter and mayonnaise. Americans should know that a favorite mâchon is a food that they habitually snub: fried pork rinds!

CHILLED CHUKAR PARTRIDGE
WITH PEARL ONIONS

MAKES 4 FIRST-COURSE SERVINGS

An elegant picnic or luncheon dish, tender light-meat chukars (young partridges)
take on the tangy and robust flavor of this wine, tomato, and coriander marinade.
Serve this dish with a crusty bread, some COUNTRY HERB AND ROQUEFORT BUTTER
(see page 132) and a light red wine, such as Beaujolais.

4 wild chukars, about 10 to 12 ounces each
(substitute farm-raised chukars, quail, lark, plover,
game pigeons, or Cornish game hens)

FOR THE HOT MARINADE:

20 small fresh pearl onions, peeled
2 tablespoons canola oil
¼ cup olive oil
1½ cups carrots, diced
750ml bottle dry white wine, such as Sauvignon Blanc
juice of 2 lemons, freshly squeezed
1 cup water
4 Italian plum tomatoes, peeled, seeded, and chopped
16 coarsely cracked black peppercorns
2 tablespoons whole coriander seeds
1 bouquet garni *(see page 3)*
salt and freshly ground pepper to taste

1   To peel the pearl onions, cut a tiny X at the base of each one, then drop them into rapidly boiling water for one minute. Drain the onions quickly and, when cool enough to handle, peel away the thin outer layer.

2   Heat the canola oil and 3 tablespoons of the olive oil in a skillet. Sauté the onions and the diced carrots together until golden brown, about 15 minutes. Add the wine, lemon juice, water, tomatoes, peppercorns, coriander seeds, and bouquet garni. Season to taste with salt and fresh pepper. Simmer, uncovered, for 20 minutes.

3 Place the chukars in a pot large enough to hold them all and pour the hot marinade mixture over them. Bring to a simmer and cook, covered, for an additional 25 minutes, then let cool slightly. Remove and discard the bouquet garni.

4 Carefully transfer the birds and the sauce to a deep bowl or other non-reactive container. Douse with the remaining tablespoon of olive oil and cover tightly with plastic wrap. Chill in the refrigerator for a minimum of two days, a maximum of four. (The flavors will deepen the longer the chukars remain in the marinade.)

5 To serve, remove the chukars from the marinade and drain (discard the marinade). Arrange them on a serving platter. With a slotted spoon, remove the pearl onions from the marinade and arrange them around the chukars as an accompaniment. Garnish with decorative sprigs of fresh herbs.

A WILD GAME PICNIC

In France, a picnic implies that every dish is served cold. Imagine a sunny bank alongside a rushing stream, blankets, and a gathering of friends.

Chilled Chukar Partridge	**Hard-boiled eggs**
Smoked Salmon Spread	**Fresh, soft cheeses**
Wild Boar Terrine	**A big jar of Dijon mustard**
Wild Duck Prosciutto	**A bowl of tiny cornichons pickles**
French Potato Salad	**Lots and lots of crusty bread**

Hot Pâté of Woodland Squirrel en Croûte with Hazelnuts

Serves 6 as an appetizer or first course

1 cup port

¼ cup minced celery

2 bay leaves

1 large sprig fresh thyme

¼ cup minced shallots

¼ cup minced carrots

3 dressed woodland squirrels, about 3 pounds

(substitute wild rabbit or hare, or game-farm rabbit)

7 ounces pork shoulder, cut into large cubes, ready to grind

½ cup crushed hazelnuts

2 tablespoons chopped fresh Italian flatleaf parsley

2 tablespoons hazelnut oil

2 tablespoons bread crumbs

2 whole eggs

salt and freshly ground pepper

8 ounces puff pastry dough, chilled (ready-made is fine)

1 egg yolk, plus 1 teaspoon cream to make an egg wash

fresh chopped parsley for garnish

For the Sauce:

2 tablespoons canola oil

¼ cup brandy

3 cups Rich Game Stock *(see page 14)*

3 tablespoons unsalted butter

1   In a glass bowl or casserole combine the port, celery, bay leaves, thyme sprig, shallots, and carrots to make a marinade. Remove all the squirrel meat from the bones (reserve and refrigerate bones). Toss meat with the marinade; cover and refrigerate for approximately 3 hours.

2   Remove the meat from the marinade. Strain the vegetables from the liquid marinade and reserve the vegetables and marinade in separate bowls, covered and refrigerated.

3   Grind the squirrel meat together with the pork shoulder to medium-coarse consistency. Place the meats in a large mixing bowl and add the reserved marinade liquid, crushed hazelnuts, parsley, hazelnut oil, bread crumbs, and the 2 eggs. Combine well with a wooden spoon. Season to taste with salt and pepper.

4   Line a baking sheet with buttered waxed or parchment paper. On a floured surface, roll out the puff pastry while still cold to form an 11x6-inch rectangle.

5   Shape the pâté meat mixture into a cylinder-shaped loaf about 9 inches long. Place it lengthwise at the long base of the pastry dough, leaving 1 inch on each side to enclose the pâté. Brush the dough edges lightly with water, then carefully roll the dough away from you to encase the pâté loaf, maintaining the cylindrical shape. Pinch and smooth the edges of the dough to seal. Place the finished loaf, seam side down, on the baking sheet. Brush the dough with the egg wash and cover loosely. Refrigerate for 1 hour before baking.

6   Preheat the oven to 350°F. To prepare the sauce, heat the canola oil in a heavy skillet. Add the reserved squirrel bones to the pan, along with the reserved marinade vegetables, and brown them over medium-high heat, approximately 15 to 20 minutes. Deglaze the pan with the brandy and add the game stock. Simmer over medium heat until the sauce is reduced by half. Strain into a smaller saucepan, then whisk in the butter. Keep very warm.

7   Bake the chilled pâté, uncovered, for 30 minutes, until golden brown. Remove from the oven and let cool slightly, about 10 minutes.

8   Have ready 6 warm first-course plates. Transfer the pâté to a cutting board and with a very sharp knife, slice it into six 1½-inch thick slices. Pour some warm sauce on each plate and place the pâté slice in the center. Garnish with chopped parsley.

RILLETTE OF
WILD RABBIT GATEAU

MAKES FOUR 3½-INCH ROUND RILLETTES, OR RAMEKINS

6 cups RENDERED DUCK FAT *(see page 140)*
1 small wild rabbit cut into 6 pieces, about 3 pounds
(substitute farm-raised rabbit, duck, goose, or pork)
4 large portobello mushrooms
6 tablespoons balsamic vinegar
6 tablespoons olive oil
¼ cup thinly sliced shallots (about 2 medium shallots)
1 tablespoon fresh minced chives
1 tablespoon fresh minced Italian flatleaf parsley
salt and freshly ground black pepper to taste

1 Place the duck fat in a pot large enough to also hold all the rabbit pieces. Melt the fat over low heat, then add the rabbit, making sure the fat covers the meat completely. Simmer gently, uncovered, for 2 hours.

2 Remove the rabbit from the fat and drain. When cool enough to handle, pull the meat from the bones with your fingers, taking care to remove any tiny, sharp bones. Discard the bones. Strain the duck fat through a fine wire mesh or chinois. Set aside and chill ¾ cup of the fat. Cover and refrigerate the remaining duck fat for later use. (Carefully covered, the remaining duck fat can be held for 2 weeks in the refrigerator or frozen for up to 6 months.)

3 Preheat the oven to 350°F. Trim the stems from the portobellos and brush them clean. Place them cap-side-up in a baking dish and drizzle evenly with the balsamic vinegar and olive oil. Season lightly with salt and pepper. Bake for 20 minutes. Remove the pan from the oven and set aside to cool.

4 In a large mixing bowl, mix the pulled rabbit meat, the reserved ¾ cup chilled duck fat, shallots, chives, and parsley, tossing with a wooden spoon or spatula. Season to taste with additional salt and pepper. Blend until the mixture becomes a coarse spread.

5 Have ready 4 ramekins, 3 to 4 inches in diameter. Cut the roasted portobello mushrooms into thin slices. Using ⅓ of the mushrooms, arrange a layer of sliced mushrooms in the bottom of the ramekin. Next, spread half the rabbit rillette

mixture into the ramekins. Add a second mushroom layer, then the remaining half of the rabbit mixture, finishing with a final layer of mushroom slices. Chill in the refrigerator for 1 hour.

6   To serve, arrange a bed of salad greens on appetizer plates. Unmold the rillette atop the greens.

MOUSSELINE
OF WILD HARE

MAKES 6 INDIVIDUAL TIMBALE APPETIZERS

*This light mousseline is a vehicle for the full, rich flavor of true
wild hare or rabbit. For this recipe, a farm-raised alternative would be too mild.
Serve with* RED CURRANT SAUCE FOR GAME *(see page 135).*

*NOTE: Making a classic mousseline need not be intimidating to the at-home chef.
The secret to achieving the right texture is the careful pressing of the meat through a
wire mesh sieve to remove any coarse bits of sinew and connective tissue called "silverskin."
Use only the large muscle meat fillets to avoid the fine, tiny bones found in wild hare.*

4 tablespoons unsalted butter, softened
12 ounces fresh, boned hare (exclude the fine-boned saddle meat)
5 ounces fresh, boned pheasant
(substitute wild rabbit for hare; substitute veal shoulder for pheasant)
4 whole eggs
2 cups heavy cream
salt and freshly ground black pepper
1 cup water
1 sprig fresh tarragon
1 medium carrot, diced into ¼-inch cubes
2 tablespoons fresh, chopped chives

1   Use 2 tablespoons of the butter to grease six 4-ounce ramekins, then refrigerate the
ramekins until they are very cold and the butter is solid.

2   Cut the meats into narrow strips. Using the finest blade of the grinder, grind the
meats together.

3   In a mixing bowl, combine the meat, eggs, and cream. Season lightly with salt and
pepper, then beat well with a wooden spoon until smooth. Using the back of the
spoon or a spatula, gradually force the mixture through a wire mesh sieve to achieve
a pastelike texture.

4   Pour the water into a small skillet or saucepan. Add 1 tablespoon of the butter and sprig of tarragon. Lightly season with salt and pepper. Bring to a boil and add the diced carrot. Simmer until all the liquid has evaporated. Remove the tarragon, place the carrot dice in a small strainer, and set aside to cool.

5   Preheat the oven to 300°F. Divide the mousseline mixture evenly among the ramekins to make 6 timbales. Smooth the tops with a spatula. Top with the diced carrots, pressing them lightly into the surface of the timbales.

6   Prepare a water bath, or *bain-marie*, by placing the filled ramekins in a shallow baking pan, then adding simmering water to surround the ramekins until the baking pan is approximately half full. Use the remaining tablespoon of soft butter to coat a sheet of tin foil large enough to cover the baking pan. Place the buttered foil over the pan and carefully seal the edges. Bake for 20 minutes or until the mousseline is firm.

7   While still hot, unmold the timbales by inverting each ramekin onto an individual plate. Surround each with a pool of RED CURRANT SAUCE FOR GAME *(see page 135)*. To finish, scatter the plate with a generous pinch of fresh chopped chives, and garnish with a bundle of 3 or 4 long, whole chives.

Spiced Terrine of Wild Turkey Leg in Aspic

Serves 8 as a first course

4 pounds wild turkey legs
(substitute chicken legs and thighs, or whole rabbit, boned)
salt and freshly ground pepper
3 whole cloves
1 large carrot, chopped
2 bay leaves
1 medium white onion, chopped
2 tablespoons fresh, grated ginger
2 juniper berries
1 cup dry white wine
2 tablespoons unflavored gelatin powder

1   Place the meat in a large soup pot and cover with enough cold water to cover the meat by 2 inches. Bring to a boil over medium heat. Reduce heat to low and simmer for 20 minutes, skimming the surface frequently with a shallow spoon to remove foam and solids from the stock.

2   After 20 minutes, add all the remaining ingredients — except the gelatin — to the pot. Simmer 1 hour.

3   Remove the meat from the pot and set aside until cool enough to handle. Remove the skin and pull the meat from bones. Discard skin and bones.

4   Continue to simmer the broth until it is reduced to 3 cups liquid, then strain it through a fine mesh strainer. Place the broth in a large saucepan.

5   Cut the turkey meat into ¾-inch cubes and add it to the saucepan with the broth. Simmer 5 minutes and correct the seasoning, adding additional salt and pepper to taste if needed.

6   Have ready a 2-quart decorative terrine mold or loaf pan. Mix the gelatin powder with 2 to 3 tablespoons of cold water to soften it. Add the gelatin mixture to the meat and broth in the saucepan; stir. Pour the contents of the saucepan into the terrine or loaf pan. Cover and chill for at least 24 hours.

7   To serve, briefly dip the terrine or loaf pan into a warm water bath, taking care to loosen the terrine from the mold, but not to melt the aspic. Invert the mold onto a platter or cutting board. Slice the terrine with a sharp knife and place the slices on individual plates, accompanied by a mixed green salad.

WINE-POACHED GREAT LAKES WALLEYE

SERVES 4

1 cup Sauvignon Blanc

2 cups water

1 tablespoon tomato paste

2 tablespoons olive oil

¼ teaspoon whole coriander seeds

¼ teaspoon juniper berries

1 sprig fresh thyme

6 sprigs fresh Italian flatleaf parsley, plus 2 tablespoons, minced, for garnish

1 bay leaf

zest of 1 lemon

2 small white onions, peeled and sliced

sea salt and freshly ground pepper

4 walleye fillets, 6 ounces each

(substitute pike or bass)

thin lemon slices

2 hard-cooked eggs, chopped, for garnish

SCRATCH-MADE TARTAR SAUCE *(see page 137)*

1   For the poaching liquid: In a saucepan combine the wine, water, tomato paste, olive oil, coriander, juniper berries, thyme, parsley sprigs, bay leaf, lemon zest, and onions. Bring to a boil and season with salt and pepper.

2   Gently add the fish fillets and return the pot to a boil. Poach the fish for 5 minutes.

3   Carefully remove the fish from the pan and place them in a shallow dish. Pour a tablespoon or two of poaching liquid over each fillet. Cover and refrigerate for at least 3 hours.

4   To serve, garnish with thin lemon slices, chopped hard-cooked eggs, and minced parsley. Serve with a ramekin of SCRATCH-MADE TARTAR SAUCE *(see page 137)* on the side.

GULF SHRIMP SALAD WITH PISTACHIOS

SERVES 4

*Meaty crawfish tails or lobster will do just as well in this
tangy seafood salad, made piquant with fresh grated horseradish and with
the unexpected addition of chopped pistachios.*

12 medium shrimp, cooked and peeled, about 1½ cups
(substitute crawfish tails or lobster)

½ cup SCRATCH-MADE MAYONNAISE *(see page 51)*
(substitute prepared mayonnaise)

2 tablespoons capers, drained and minced

2 tablespoons fresh horseradish, finely grated
(or good-quality prepared horseradish)

2 tablespoons unsalted pistachios, finely chopped

1 teaspoon chopped fresh chives

1 teaspoon chopped fresh dill

salt and freshly ground pepper to taste

TOMATO FONDUE *(see page 134)*

1   Slice or coarsely chop the shrimp *(or other shellfish)*. Toss with the remaining
    ingredients and finish by seasoning to taste with salt and fresh pepper.

2   Cover the mixture with plastic wrap and chill for at least 2 hours before serving.
    Serve with a dollop of TOMATO FONDUE alongside.

> "The Roman fish market, well stocked and handsomely laid out as
> it was, gives us only a faint idea of the Roman's passion for
> fish…When a really huge fish appeared in the market, no one
> dared buy it for fear of incurring the emperor's displeasure."
>
> —TOUSSAINT-SAMAT,
> FROM *HISTORY OF FOOD*

Marinated Wild Mushrooms with Three Spices

Serves 4

A side dish to enhance any chilled game appetizer, such as pâté.

**8 ounces each chanterelles, hedgehog, baby cepes,
and horn of plenty mushrooms (2 pounds total)**
(substitute domestic, shiitake or crimini mushrooms)
¾ cup extra virgin olive oil
1 garlic clove, finely minced
1 sprig fresh thyme or ½ teaspoon dried thyme
½ bay leaf
6 peppercorns, lightly crushed
½ teaspoon ground coriander
½ teaspoon fennel seeds
6 parsley sprigs

1   Bring a pan of lightly salted water to a boil. Drop in the chanterelles and blanch for 3 minutes, then drain the mushrooms well. Repeat this step for each type of mushroom. Combine the mushrooms together in a deep bowl.

2   In a large saucepan bring the oil and all the remaining ingredients to a simmer. Cover and cook over very low heat for 15 minutes.

3   Pour the simmering marinade over the wild mushrooms and let the mixture cool to room temperature. Cover and refrigerate for 3 days, tossing the mixture daily.

4   To serve, drain the mushrooms from the marinade and divide evenly among 4 small bowls, reserving some marinade to drizzle on top.

Country Gougere
or Hot Cheese Puffs

MAKES ABOUT 2 DOZEN GOUGERE

*Nothing is better with a fine Cabernet Sauvignon
than hot gougere straight from the oven.*

1 cup water
½ cup unsalted butter
¼ teaspoon salt
1 cups sifted all-purpose flour
5 whole eggs, room temperature
½ cup grated imported Gruyère cheese

1   Preheat the oven to 350°F. Line a cookie sheet with waxed or parchment paper.

2   In a heavy saucepan, bring the water, butter, and salt to a boil. Add all the flour and stir vigorously with a wooden spoon until smooth, continuing to cook over medium heat, stirring, for 5 minutes. Transfer to a large mixing bowl or the bowl of an electric mixer.

3   Using a paddle attachment—or a wide spatula if mixing the batter manually—beat in the eggs one at a time. Add the cheese and beat for an additional minute.

4   Pipe the batter through the star tip of a pastry bag, or drop it by rounded table-spoons, onto the cookie sheet. Bake until puffed and golden brown, 15 to 18 minutes. Serve warm as an appetizer or as a garnish for bowls of hot soup.

WILD DUCK PROSCIUTTO

Use thin slivers of this pungent, salt-cured duck breast just as you would Italian prosciutto ham — in pastas, on pizzas, in salads or served with fruit.

1 whole boneless breast of Muscovy duck
1 teaspoon juniper berries
1 teaspoon minced dried dates
1 teaspoon coriander seeds
2 tablespoons chopped fresh sage leaves
coarsely ground black pepper
2 cups rock salt

1   Using a razor-sharp knife, trim any excess fat from the duck breast, leaving the layer of breast skin intact. Pat the breast dry with a kitchen towel.

2   Put the juniper berries, dates, and coriander seeds in a food processor or spice grinder and reduce to a powder. Add the chopped sage and grind again to combine, about 30 seconds.

3   Season the duck with the black pepper and coat on all sides with the spice mixture.

4   Pour a layer of rock salt in the bottom of a bowl or glass pan just large enough to hold the duck breast. Put the duck breast on top of the salt layer, then cover with the remaining salt. Use as much salt as necessary to cover the breast completely. Cover and cure in the refrigerator for 16 hours.

5   Pull the duck breast from the cure and rinse off any remaining rock salt. Bind the breast with kitchen twine and hang in the refrigerator to dry for 14 days.

"Hunting led to technology. Man had to use cunning
and ingenuity to compensate for his vulnerability and his
inferiority to his prey in strength, number and sense of smell.
It was to get game that he first made tools."

—TOUSSAINT-SAMAT, FROM *HISTORY OF FOODS*

Salads, Vinaigrette Variations, & Dressings

Variations on Classic Vinaigrette

CHAMPAGNE VINAIGRETTE

MAKES 2 CUPS

2 egg yolks
½ cup Champagne vinegar
1 cup canola oil
1 cup extra virgin olive oil
2 tablespoons chopped fresh Italian flatleaf parsley
salt and freshly ground pepper

Method #1: Whisk together the egg yolks and vinegar. Drizzle in the oils, whisking constantly, to make an emulsion. Add parsley and salt and pepper to taste.

Method #2: Place egg yolks and vinegar in the bowl of a food processor. Pulse to blend. Slowly pour in the oils with the motor running to make an emulsion. Add parsley, salt, and pepper, and pulse once more to blend.

TRUFFLE OIL VINAIGRETTE

MAKES ½ CUP

1 tablespoon red wine vinegar
1 tablespoon Spanish sherry vinegar
2 teaspoons water
5 tablespoons truffle-infused olive oil (white or black truffles)
salt and freshly ground pepper

Whisk vinegars and water together, then slowly whisk in truffle oil. Season to taste.

Pecan Vinaigrette

Makes 2 cups

1½ cups pecan oil
⅓ cup red wine vinegar
1 tablespoon prepared whole grain mustard
½ teaspoon fresh minced garlic
2 tablespoons toasted chopped pecans
salt and freshly ground pepper

Whisk together the vinegar, mustard, and garlic. Slowly drizzle in the oil, whisking constantly to make an emulsion. Season to taste with salt and pepper and blend in the pecans.

Sweet and Sour Maple Vinaigrette

Makes 3 cups

2 medium shallots, minced
2 teaspoons minced fresh garlic *(optional)*
½ cup prepared Dijon mustard
¼ cup Vermont maple syrup
1 tablespoon sugar
¼ cup white balsamic vinegar
¼ cup red wine vinegar
2½ cups canola oil
½ cup chopped fresh Italian flatleaf parsley
salt and freshly ground pepper

1   Combine shallots, garlic, mustard, maple syrup, sugar, and vinegars in the bowl of a food processor. Pulse for 10 seconds.

2   With the motor running, slowly drizzle in the oil to make an emulsion.

3   Add the parsley and adjust the seasoning. Cover and keep, refrigerated, for up to 10 days.

Green Lentil and Apple Salad in Curry Vinaigrette

Serves 6 as an appetizer or side dish

1½ cups dried French green lentils

1 medium white onion

3 whole cloves

2 bay leaves

1 teaspoon salt

freshly ground pepper to taste

3 tablespoons prepared Dijon mustard

2 tablespoons cider vinegar

5 tablespoons extra virgin olive oil

5 tablespoons canola oil

2 teaspoons curry powder

1 Granny Smith apple, cored, peeled, and diced

2 shallots, minced

2 tablespoons chopped fresh Italian flatleaf parsley

1 Put the lentils in a large, heavy saucepan and cover with 5 cups cold water. Peel the onion and cut it in half. Stud one onion half with the cloves and add it to the saucepan along with the bay leaves and salt. Mince the other onion half and reserve.

2 Bring the pot to a boil and simmer until the lentils are tender, but still firm and a bit chewy, about 20 to 25 minutes. Drain the lentils when done and rinse with cold water.

3 In a mixing bowl, whisk together the mustard, vinegar, olive and canola oils, and the curry powder. Toss the drained lentils in the vinaigrette, along with the diced apple, the minced onion and shallots, and the parsley. Season to taste with salt and pepper. Serve chilled.

The European tradition of eating the salad as a final course is a fading tradition. Today even the French are more likely to eat their salad as a first or second course as opposed to the last. Chef Blondin defends the old ways — it is better for digestion, says he, both an elegant and healthful way to end a meal.

Garlic and Red Onion Dressing

Makes 3 cups

3 egg yolks
2 teaspoons minced fresh garlic
¼ cup red wine vinegar, or juice from jarred capers
2 tablespoons prepared Dijon mustard
½ cup finely diced red bermuda onion
1 cup olive oil
½ cup canola oil
salt and freshly ground pepper

1   Combine egg yolks, garlic, vinegar or caper juice, mustard, and diced onion in the bowl of a food processor. Pulse for 10 seconds.
2   With the motor running, slowly drizzle in the oils to make an emulsion. Season to taste with salt and pepper.

Basil-Infused Oil

Makes 1 cup

*Create this brilliant green oil to give a burst of flavor and color
to salads or a decorative splash to a finished platter before it goes on the table.*

8 ounces fresh basil leaves
1 cup olive or sunflower oil

1   Bring a large pot of salted water to a full boil. Drop in the basil leaves and blanch for just a few seconds. Drain the leaves and plunge them into a bowl of ice water. Drain again and dry completely on kitchen towels. (If the leaves are wet, the infused oil will be cloudy.)
2   Place the leaves and the oil in the bowl of a food processor and puree until very smooth.
3   Strain the oil through a cheesecloth or very fine wire mesh and store in the refrigerator for up to one week.

HAZELNUT-ENDIVE SALAD
WITH GOAT CHEESE

SERVES 4

A grilled breast of game bird goes perfectly atop this tangy salad.

4 large heads belgian endive
½ cup hazelnut oil
1 teaspoon prepared Dijon mustard
1 tablespoon Cabernet wine vinegar *(or other strong red vinegar)*
4 tablespoons fresh goat cheese (Montrachet)
salt and freshly ground pepper

1   Trim the root ends of the endive and separate the leaves. Set aside in a bowl for tossing.

2   In a small bowl, whisk together the mustard and hazelnut oil until thick.

3   Heat the red wine vinegar and quickly whisk it with the oil and mustard. Season to taste with salt and pepper and pour the warm vinaigrette over the endive. Toss, divide onto 4 salad plates, and garnish with crumbled goat cheese.

> "I ground black pepper over the potatoes and moistened the bread in the olive oil.
> After the first heavy draft of beer I drank and ate very slowly.
> When the pommes a l'huile were gone I ordered another serving…"
>
> —ERNEST HEMINGWAY

FRENCH POTATO SALAD

SERVES 4

2 pounds potatoes (redskin or Yukon Gold) peeled and cooked
3 hard-cooked eggs
1 tablespoon minced shallots
fresh shaved truffles (if available) *(substitute 2 tablespoons chopped fresh chives)*
½ cup TRUFFLE OIL VINAIGRETTE *(see page 46)*

Toss the first 4 ingredients with ½ cup Truffle Oil Vinaigrette. Chill before serving.

SCRATCH-MADE MAYONNAISE

MAKES 5 CUPS

*A tangy enhancement to chilled game meats, on sandwiches,
or as a base for salad dressings. Authentic mayonnaise is simple to make
and far superior to ready-made versions!*

4 egg yolks
½ cup prepared French Dijon mustard
4 cups vegetable oil
3 tablespoons warm red wine vinegar
salt and freshly ground pepper to taste

1   Place the yolks in the bowl of a food processor. Pulse for 30 seconds.

2   Add the mustard and pulse again to blend thoroughly. Slowly drizzle in 2 cups of the oil while the motor is running. Add the warm vinegar, pulse for 30 seconds to blend, then drizzle in the remaining 2 cups oil while the motor is running to make a thick emulsion.

3   Season to taste with salt and pepper. Place in an airtight glass container and chill. Keeps in the refrigerator for up to 5 days.

A RARE MUSTARD

A delicacy still rarely available outside France is a mustard called "mout de raisin." It is a deep purple mustard made from the fermented dregs taken from the bottom of red wine barrels, which gives the mustard its special strong wine flavor. It can be used on meats or in vinaigrettes and will impart a dramatic purple color to any dish to which it's added. If you or a friend are on the way to France, here's a simple souvenir worth seeking out. "Bring me a jar of mout de raisin!"

❧

Two things in life are essential: to give good dinners
and to keep on fair terms with women.
— Talleyrand

Main Courses
Wild Game Meats

Grilled Venison Tenderloins Wrapped in Double-Smoked Bacon

Serves 4 as a main course

*A "double-smoked" bacon will perfectly season venison tenderloins
and keep the meat moist as it grills over hot coals or on a range-top grill.
If "double-smoked" isn't available, use the smokiest you can find.
Whole Grain Mustard Spätzle (see page 111) makes a perfect side dish.*

16 thin slices of double-smoked bacon

16 large fresh sage leaves

4 venison tenderloins; thick, cylindrical cuts if possible (about 6 ounces each)

(substitute wild boar, elk, or pork tenderloin)

freshly ground black pepper

2 tablespoons canola oil

2 tablespoons unsalted butter

good kitchen twine

1   If grilling outdoors, prepare coals. If grilling on the range-top, lightly oil the grid and heat just prior to preparing the tenderloins.

2   On a cutting board, place 4 slices of bacon lengthwise with edges overlapping, to make a rectangle. Repeat until you have 4 rectangles, one for each tenderloin.

3   Press a fresh sage leaf on each slice of bacon, then place the tenderloin atop the sage leaves. Season with freshly ground pepper, then carefully roll the tenderloins inside the bacon to achieve a cylindrical shape. Secure each with 3 or 4 lengths of kitchen twine and brush with canola oil.

4   Grill the tenderloins for about 4 minutes total for rare to medium-rare doneness, rolling them constantly with tongs so that they cook evenly.

5   When done, quickly clip away the twine and slice each tenderloin into medallions, ½–1 inch thick. Arrange the slices on the plate and top each with a large pat of butter.

ROASTED RACK OF VENISON
WITH CARAWAY CRUST

SERVES 4

*Any rack of rib chops will cook more evenly if "frenched," a technique that
leaves the fatty ends of the individual chop bones trimmed completely clean.
Ask an experienced butcher to "french" your venison rack for you if you aren't familiar
with the process. This recipe will also work with a whole boneless tenderloin of venison,
veal, or pork, but cut the estimated cooking time in half at each step.*

2 to 2½-pound rack of venison, "frenched"
(substitute rack of boar, veal, or lamb)
salt and freshly ground pepper
1 tablespoon canola oil
½ tablespoon unsalted butter
¾ cup fine, dry bread crumbs
2 tablespoons whole caraway seeds
2 tablespoons freshly ground caraway seeds
1 tablespoon fresh garlic, minced
1 tablespoon chopped fresh Italian flatleaf parsley
1 egg yolk
¼ cup prepared Dijon mustard

1   Preheat the oven to 350°F. Season the venison on all sides with salt and pepper.
    Heat the oil and butter together in a heavy, ovenproof skillet large enough to hold
    the rack.

2   Sear the rack on all sides until it is a rich brown color, about 5 minutes. Place the
    skillet in the oven and bake for 5 minutes. Remove the skillet from the oven and let
    rest for 20 minutes.

3   Toss the bread crumbs with the caraway seeds, ground caraway, garlic, and parsley.

4   Beat the egg yolk together with the mustard. Brush the meat with the egg-mustard
    mixture, then roll the rack in the bread crumb mixture to entirely coat the meat.

5   Place the rack in the skillet and return it to the pre-heated oven. Roast for 8 to 10
    minutes for medium-rare; about 12 minutes for medium.

6   To serve, use a sharp, serrated carving knife to slice the rack into individual chops.

Venison Tenderloin with Mustard Sauce and Wild Mushrooms

Serves 4

*A mellow mustard crème sauce and gently sautéed mushrooms make
for a beautiful—and remarkably easy—presentation for your fine tenderloin
of venison. Hearty wild mushrooms will do the meat proper justice,
but if none are available, fresh and firm domestic
mushrooms are a good substitute.*

12 ounces fresh wild mushrooms such as chanterelles, porcini, oyster

4½ tablespoons unsalted butter, softened

1 clove garlic, finely chopped

1 cup heavy cream

1 teaspoon whole mustard seeds

2 teaspoons imported prepared whole grain mustard

salt and freshly ground black pepper to taste

2 teaspoons freshly squeezed lemon juice

1½–2 pound tenderloin of venison, sliced into 16, 1½–2 ounce medallions

(substitute veal)

1 to 2 tablespoons olive oil

minced fresh chives to garnish, about 2 tablespoons

1   Clean the mushrooms well. Leave whole if bite-sized; if not, chop coarsely. In a skillet, melt 1 tablespoon of butter. Add the garlic and mushrooms and sauté until the mushrooms have released their juices and most of the liquid has evaporated. Transfer the mixture to a separate dish, cover, and keep warm.

2   Add the cream and the mustard seeds to the skillet and bring to a boil. Simmer 3 to 4 minutes to reduce the cream until slightly thickened. Lower the heat and add the prepared mustard and the remaining 3½ tablespoons of butter, cut into small pieces. Quickly whisk the mixture, being very careful not to allow the sauce to return to a boil. Remove the pan from the heat and season with salt and pepper. Add the lemon juice a little at a time, until you are pleased with the degree of tartness. Cover and set aside.

3 Season the venison medallions lightly with salt and freshly ground black pepper. In a second skillet, heat the olive oil. Sear the venison medallions in the hot pan for approximately 30 seconds per side for medium rare; just a bit longer for a greater degree of doneness.

4 To serve, pile ¼ of the sautéed mushrooms in the center of each dinner plate. Place 4 venison medallions around the mushrooms. Carefully warm the mustard créme sauce and spoon it over the medallions. Garnish each plate with minced fresh chives.

GRILLED VENISON LOIN IN HOT CAYENNE MARINADE

For indoor or outdoor grilling. A spoonful of cayenne pepper adds heat to this marinade. Serve with rich POTATOES FONDANTES *(see page 107).*

4 tablespoons prepared Dijon mustard

4 tablespoons red wine vinegar

1 teaspoon ground cayenne pepper

¼ teaspoon salt

¾ cup canola oil

2 teaspoons fresh thyme leaves, chopped

4 cuts of venison sirloin, 7 ounces each

(substitute wild boar or veal, or pork)

1   Whisk together first 6 ingredients to make a vinaigrette marinade.

2   Toss the sirloins thoroughly in the marinade, then cover tightly with plastic wrap and refrigerate overnight, or a minimum of 12 hours.

3   Remove the meat from the marinade and drain. Cook outdoors over very hot coals, or indoors on a hot range-top grill. Cook for 3 minutes per side to sear, then push the meat to a cooler spot on the grill to achieve desired doneness, about 6 to 8 minutes total for medium-rare.

Venison Loin, Hunter Style

Serves 4 as an entrée

These venison loin steaks are traditionally served atop a thick slice of well-toasted garlic bread to absorb the rich wine sauce and pan juices.

6 tablespoons unsalted butter

3 tablespoons walnut oil

4 7-ounce boneless loin steaks of venison, about 1-inch thick

(substitute elk, veal, beef, or pork)

4 medium shallots, minced

4 ounces mushrooms, minced

1 cup dry white wine

1 cup Rich Game Stock *(see page 14)*

1 tablespoon tomato puree

1 tablespoon buerre manie: combine equal parts of soft butter with flour to form a smooth paste to thicken the sauce

salt and freshly ground black pepper

2 tablespoons minced Italian flatleaf parsley

optional: garlic toast

1   In a deep skillet large enough to hold all the loin steaks, heat 3 tablespoons butter and the walnut oil over high heat. Have a warm serving platter ready. Add the loin steaks to the pan and sear on both sides to the desired doneness, 2 to 3 minutes per side for medium-rare. Quickly transfer the meat to the warm platter.

2   Hunter Sauce: Add the remaining 3 tablespoons of butter to the pan. Add the shallots and mushrooms and sauté until light golden brown, about 5 minutes.

3   Add the wine to the pan and bring the mixture to a boil. Reduce the liquid by ⅔. Add the game stock and tomato puree and mix well. Stir in the buerre manie and simmer an additional 5 minutes until the sauce thickens. Check the seasoning and add salt and pepper to taste.

4   Return the loins to the pan and turn them in the sauce briefly to coat and warm them, without cooking them further.

5   To serve, arrange the loin steaks on the serving platter and pour the Hunter Sauce on top. Place each on a slice of garlic toast, if you like. Sprinkle generously with minced parsley.

Sweet and Spicy
Venison Meatloaf

Serves 6 to 8

A juicy meatloaf to serve with a steaming bowl of
Garlic and Rosemary Mashed Potatoes *(see page 105)*.

2 pounds venison (leg meat)

12 ounces pork shoulder

3 ounces pork or chicken liver (optional)

3 ounces bacon

3 tablespoons honey

2 tablespoons whole grain mustard

3 tablespoons prepared ketchup

2 tablespoons brandy

1 tablespoon canola oil

½ tablespoon unsalted butter

1 large onion, diced

2 jalapeño peppers, seeded and diced

1 tablespoon olive oil

8 ounces fresh button mushrooms, sliced

salt and freshly ground black pepper to taste

1 beaten egg

¼ cup dried bread crumbs

1 teaspoon fresh, chopped tarragon (or ½ teaspoon dried)

1 teaspoon fresh, chopped Italian flatleaf parsley

1 teaspoon fresh, chopped sage (or ½ teaspoon dried)

½ teaspoon cayenne pepper

1   Grind together the venison, pork, liver, and bacon. Set aside.

2   Whisk together the honey, mustard, ketchup, and brandy. Set aside for glazing the meatloaf.

3 Heat the canola oil and butter in a small skillet. Cook the onion and jalapeño pepper in the skillet until lightly brown, about 5 minutes. Transfer to a small bowl. In the same skillet, heat the olive oil and sauté the mushrooms until tender and light brown, about 5 minutes. Season lightly with salt and pepper and set aside.

4 Preheat the oven to 350°F. In a large mixing bowl, use a spatula to combine the ground meats, egg, bread crumbs, tarragon, parsley, sage, sautéed onions, peppers, and mushrooms, and cayenne. Pre-cook a small patty of the meatloaf in a skillet or microwave to test the seasoning. Add salt and pepper if needed.

5 Line a large flat baking sheet or jelly roll pan (with sides at least one inch high) with waxed or parchment paper. Shape the mixture into a smooth loaf in the center of the pan, about 3 inches wide by 10 inches long. Place in the preheated oven.

6 Every 8 minutes, brush the loaf with the honey-mustard glaze. Bake for a total of 35 to 40 minutes. Let rest for 10 minutes.

7 To serve, transfer the loaf to a decorative platter and serve with a steaming bowl of GARLIC AND ROSEMARY MASHED POTATOES (*see page 105*).

A GAME MEAT SUPPER
SUITABLE FOR A SUMMER NIGHT

Green Lentil and Apple Salad in Curry Vinaigrette

Wild Boar Terrine with Caramelized Fennel

**Venison Loin, Hunter Style,
with Whole Grain Mustard Spätzle**

Dark Chocolate Tart accompanied by a hearty glass of port

"This meal," says Blondin, "would demand a Cabernet Sauvignon—a very sharp wine with true game and a milder Cabernet with farm-raised game."

Braised Venison Shank a L'Orange

Serves 4

*Plenty of wine and citrus add a tangy sweetness and depth of flavor
to this hearty, rustic dish. Serve with crusty bread and a
light red wine such as Beaujolais or Pinot Noir.*

4 tablespoons canola oil

3 tablespoons unsalted butter

2 venison shanks, about 1 pound each

(substitute veal, lamb, chamois, or mutton)

1 white onion, peeled and halved, with a whole clove inserted in each half

3 carrots, peeled and diced

2 turnips, peeled and diced

3 tender celery stalks from the heart, diced

4 ounces smoked ham, cut into large chunks

3 cups of dry white wine, such as Sauvignon Blanc

5 plum tomatoes, peeled, seeded, and chopped

1 bouquet garni *(see page 3)*

rind from two oranges, cut into slivers

salt and freshly ground pepper to taste

juice of one lemon

juice of one orange

12 small new potatoes, peeled

¼ cup chopped fresh Italian flatleaf parsley

1 Heat the oil and the butter together in a large, heavy, covered skillet or Dutch oven. Brown the shanks until golden on all sides.

2 Add the onion, carrots, turnips, celery, and ham. Toss to combine, then cover the pan and cook over medium-low heat for 10 minutes.

3 Add the wine, tomatoes, bouquet garni, and orange rind. Season with salt and pepper and simmer, covered, for 1 hour.

4 Add the new potatoes to the pan, pressing them so that they are partially covered in pan juices. Add a little water if necessary. Cover and simmer an additional 25 minutes.

5   The meat should be fork-tender when done. Remove the shanks to a deep serving platter and place the potatoes around them. Strain the remaining pan juices; discard the vegetables and bouquet garni. Return the liquid to the casserole and add the orange and lemon juice. Bring to a boil and reduce slightly. Check the seasoning, then pour the sauce over the venison shanks. Garnish with chopped parsley.

CHEF BLONDIN ON POTS AND PANS

Most important for a well-equipped kitchen is a proper assortment of sauté pans. When Chef Blondin takes charge of a kitchen his first command is "throw out the aluminum!" A pan with an aluminum surface is reactive to acidic ingredients like tomatoes and wine and can lend a bitter or metallic taste to your finished dish. Far better to use pans of heavy stainless steel, cast iron, or tin-lined copper.

Chef Paul Bocuse has the finest collection of pots that Blondin has ever seen, including a copper roasting pan with big bronze handles so wide and heavy that it took two men to carry it.

But what is Blondin's most important tool? "My big rubber spatula," he says. "I hate waste."

CHEF'S COPPER POT CLEANER

"Every dishwasher in France knows this recipe," says Chef Blondin.
Simple ingredients make a natural and non-toxic cleaner
to shine your fine copper pots.

3 tablespoons fresh-squeezed lemon juice

¼ cup sea salt

3 egg whites

½ cup flour

Combine the lemon juice and salt. Whisk in the egg whites. Stir in the flour to bind.

Apply some of the cleaner to a very soft dry cloth and briskly rub over the surface of the pot. Wait a minute or two, then polish.

Pot-Roasted Venison Sirloin Tips with Yukon Golds

Serves 4 to 6

Serve this earthy stew directly from the casserole at the table.
BRAISED BELGIAN ENDIVE WITH CHESTNUTS
is a perfect side dish (see page 127).

¼ cup olive oil
2 tablespoons unsalted butter
4 venison leg loin steaks, about 8 ounces each
(substitute beef sirloin tips)
2 medium white onions, minced (about 2 cups)
2 carrots, peeled and chopped
1 cup dry white wine
¼ cup tomato paste
1 bouquet garni *(see page 3)*
salt and freshly ground pepper to taste
4 large Yukon Gold potatoes, peeled and cut into thick slices

1   Heat the oil and butter together in a large, heavy, covered casserole or Dutch oven. Brown the meat on all sides over high heat, then transfer it to a platter and cover to keep warm.

2   Add the onion and carrots to the pan and cook until soft, about 10 minutes.

3   Return the meat to the pan and add the wine, tomato paste, and bouquet garni. Season lightly with salt and pepper.

4   Layer the sliced potatoes over the meat, cover, and simmer for 1 hour or until the meat is fork-tender.

5   To serve, remove the bouquet garni and season with additional salt and pepper to taste.

GRILLED WILD RABBIT
WITH HAM-PISTACHIO STUFFING

SERVES 4

4 tablespoons pistachio oil

2 tablespoons shelled, unsalted pistachios, coarsely crushed

8 ounces cooked, smoked ham

1 rabbit liver, or 1 large chicken liver

7 tablespoons heavy cream

2 whole eggs

2 teaspoons fresh, chopped tarragon leaves

1 teaspoon brandy

1 teaspoon Marsala

salt and freshly ground black pepper to taste

1 whole young rabbit, about 1½ to 2 pounds,
cleaned with cavity prepared for stuffing

1   In a small skillet heat one tablespoon of the pistachio oil. Add the crushed pistachios and toss over medium heat until the nuts are slightly browned and roasted. Remove the pistachios from the pan immediately and set aside to cool.

2   Finely grind the ham and liver together. In a mixing bowl, combine the ground meat with the cream, eggs, tarragon, brandy, and Marsala. Season with salt and pepper and mix with a wooden spoon until smooth. Blend in the roasted pistachios.

3   Place all the stuffing inside the rabbit—as you would stuff poultry—and tie the rabbit securely with several lengths of kitchen twine so that the stuffing will not spill out as the rabbit is grilled. Prepare a charcoal grill, or preheat a range-top grill to medium-high.

4   Season the rabbit on all sides with salt and pepper, then brush generously with pistachio oil. Grill the rabbit, turning frequently and basting with additional oil, for about 30 minutes.

5   When done, place the rabbit on a cutting board and carefully remove the twine. Scoop out the stuffing and spoon it onto four individual dinner plates. Carve the rabbit into quarters and place one piece atop the stuffing on each plate.

Black Bear Rump Roast Stuffed with Madeira Prunes

Serves 6 to 8 as a main course

A rich, hearty meat entrée served right out of the cooking pot
for a rustic presentation.

1 pound pitted prunes
3 cups Madeira
½ cup unsalted butter
3½- to 4-pound rump of black bear
(substitute wild boar, beef, pork, or veal)
3 carrots, peeled and sliced
1 stalk celery, sliced
salt and freshly ground black pepper to taste
3 thick slices smoked bacon
18 small new potatoes, peeled

1   Soak the prunes in the Madeira for 12 hours, or overnight.

2   Melt half the butter (4 tablespoons) in a Dutch oven or covered skillet deep enough to hold the roast. Over high heat, brown the roast on all sides, about 6 minutes. Add the carrots and celery; season with salt and pepper. Reduce heat to low, cover the pan and cook for 45 minutes, adding no liquid to the pan at this stage.

3   Remove the meat from the pan and let cool. Strain the pan juices and return them to the pan, discarding the vegetables.

4   Drain the prunes and reserve the Madeira. With a sharp knife, carve a ½-inch-thick slice from the flattest side of the roast. This slice will serve as a "lid" for the stuffing. Carefully carve out the center portion of the roast to make a large cavity to hold the prunes, leaving the bottom and sides of the intact roast about one inch thick. Mince the meat carved from the center of the roast with the bacon; mix together. Add this mixture to the Dutch oven or skillet containing the reserved pan juices. Season lightly with salt and pepper to taste.

5   Stuff the roast with the drained prunes and place the meat "lid" on top, securing it with a few long toothpicks or bamboo skewers, leaving the ends protruding for easy removal when the roast is done. Return the roast to the Dutch oven or skillet, placing it on top of the minced meat and bacon mixture. Arrange the peeled new potatoes around the roast. Cover and simmer over low heat for 1 hour.

6   While the roast cooks, reduce the reserved Madeira to 1 cup in a heavy saucepan.

7   To serve, remove the toothpicks from the roast and pour the reduced Madeira over it. Bring the roast to the table and serve directly from the cooking pan.

THE SAUTEUSE VERSUS THE SAUTOIRE

There is an important distinction between a sauté pan with slightly flared sides, a "sauteuse," and one with straight vertical sides, a "sautoire". The classic sautoire, most widely used by French chefs, is two or three inches deep so that food can be tossed and well-coated with fats and pan juices. It is used for cooking meat, fish, and poultry dishes that are often finished in the oven—a sautoire transfers quickly from the stove top to a hot oven.

The sauteuse, on the other hand, is more likely to be used for cooking vegetables—but the two are, in fact, interchangeable as long as they are of good quality and get the job done well.

Both are different from a simple frying pan which, as a rule, is smaller and shallower. A traditional American cast iron skillet, wide and well-seasoned, makes a great sautoire.

GRILLED CARIBOU CHOPS
WITH GARLIC AND CARDAMOM

SERVES 4

Aromatic green cardamom adds a spicy dimension
to these garlicky chops. Delicious, grilled indoors or out.

4 thick caribou chops, 10–12 ounces each
(substitute wild boar, venison, or pork chops)
1 cup olive oil
juice of 1 lemon
2 bay leaves
4 large cloves fresh garlic, minced
2 tablespoons crushed green cardamom pods
salt and freshly ground pepper

1   In a bowl whisk together the olive oil, lemon juice, bay leaves, garlic, and cardamom to make a marinade. Season to taste with freshly ground pepper.

2   Place the chops in a shallow glass dish and cover with the marinade. Cover the dish and refrigerate overnight.

3   Prepare hot coals for grilling. Remove the chops from the marinade and season on both sides with salt.

4   Grill no more than 5 minutes on each side for medium-rare, 1 or 2 minutes longer for medium.

BRAISED WILD BOAR CHOPS
WITH POTATOES AND SWEET ONIONS

MAKES 4 SERVINGS

3 ounces canola oil

5 plum tomatoes, peeled, seeded, and chopped

6 Yukon Gold potatoes, thickly sliced

2 cups RICH CHICKEN STOCK *(see page 16)*, or canned, unsalted chicken stock

2 sprigs fresh thyme

1 teaspoon dried sage

salt and freshly ground black pepper

4 thick-cut wild boar chops, bone-in, about 12 ounces each

(substitute venison, elk, or pork chops)

1 ounce unsalted butter

3 medium yellow onions, minced

1   Heat half the oil in a large skillet over medium-high heat and cook the tomatoes until they are very soft, about 10 minutes. Add the potatoes, chicken stock, thyme, and sage; season lightly with salt and pepper. Cover and simmer over low heat for 20 minutes. Remove from heat.

2   Season the meat on all sides with salt and freshly ground pepper. Heat the remaining oil and the butter in another skillet and brown the chops quickly over high heat, 1 to 2 minutes per side.

3   Add the minced onions to the meat, lower the heat to medium, and continue cooking until the onions are golden, approximately 7 to 10 minutes.

4   Remove the chops from the pan and place them on top of the potato mixture. Scrape the cooked onions and any pan drippings over the chops. Cover and simmer for about 2 minutes, until hot. Finish with salt and fresh pepper to taste.

Buffalo Brochettes

Makes 4 servings

Char-grilling brings out the best in flavorful buffalo steaks.
These brochettes are a festive dish, suitable for a midsummer barbecue,
or an elegant dinner any time of year. Serve with the finest
of Cabernet Sauvignons.

For the Marinade:

2 cups dry red wine

2 medium onions, chopped

2 carrots, chopped

4 shallots, chopped

1 tablespoon fresh thyme leaves, minced

2 bay leaves

16 black peppercorns, cracked

6 whole cloves

2 ounces brandy

½ teaspoon kosher salt

1½ pounds of buffalo cut into 2-inch cubes (ribeye, filet, or top round cuts)

(substitute black bear, beef, or pork)

5 stalks celery, peeled

1   Thoroughly combine all the marinade ingredients.

2   Put the buffalo cubes in the marinade and toss well to coat. Cover and refrigerate for at least 24 hours.

3   Drain the meat and dry each piece carefully. Cut the celery stalks into 1-inch pieces. Place the meat cubes on metal skewers, alternating with pieces of celery.

4   Broil under high heat, or over hot coals, turning often to brown the meat evenly. Cook for approximately 5 minutes for rare to medium-rare.

Stilton-Stuffed Roast
of Wild Sheep Shoulder

Serves 4

5 ounces English Stilton cheese, crumbled

salt and freshly ground black pepper to taste

1 shoulder of wild sheep, boned (about 3 pounds)

(substitute venison, wild boar, pork loin, or leg of lamb)

5 ounces veal shoulder, cubed

3 ounces pork loin, cubed

1 cup cooked couscous

2 tablespoons chopped fresh Italian flatleaf parsley, plus 1 tablespoon for garnish

2 tablespoons fresh chopped tarragon leaves

2 cloves fresh garlic, minced

2 tablespoons Marsala

2 tablespoons canola oil

2 tablespoons unsalted butter

4 plum tomatoes, peeled, seeded, and halved

good kitchen twine

1   Preheat the oven to 400°F. Coarsely grind together the veal and pork. In a mixing bowl, combine the ground meats, couscous, parsley, tarragon, garlic, and Marsala. Add the crumbled Stilton, season with salt and pepper to taste, and mix well.

2   Have ready 6 to 8 lengths of kitchen twine. Spread the boned roast open on a work surface. Place the stuffing in the deep-cut cavities of the boned roast. Roll the roast into as round a shape as possible, making sure all the stuffing is enclosed. Tie several lengths of twine around the roast, finishing with one length that secures the roast from end to end.

3   In an ovenproof skillet large enough to hold the roast, heat the oil and butter. Quickly sear the roast on all sides, turning and basting until evenly browned, about 3 to 5 minutes total.

4   Place the skillet in the oven. Continue to baste and turn the roast often, baking for a total of 35 minutes. Remove the pan from the oven and add the tomatoes, basting again with pan juices. Return the roast to the oven for an additional 10 minutes to finish.

5   Transfer the roast to a serving platter and remove the twine. Arrange the roasted tomatoes around it and spoon the pan juices over the platter. Garnish with additional chopped parsley. Carve at table.

Pan-Seared Saddle
of Young Hare
in Beaujolais Nouveau

A bubbling pan of Country French Scalloped Potatoes *(see page 106)*
makes a perfect accompaniment to this meaty dish rich with red wine.

2 cups Beaujolais Nouveau
4 small shallots, or 2 medium, minced
3 tablespoons Rich Game Stock *(see page 14)***, or use beef stock**
1 tablespoon buerre manie: equal parts soft butter
and flour mixed to a smooth paste

salt and freshly ground black pepper
2 tablespoons unsalted butter
2 tablespoons canola oil
4 saddles of young hare, 10 ounces each, bone-in
(substitute venison loin, beef tenderloin, veal tenderloin)
1 teaspoon chopped fresh tarragon leaves
1 teaspoon chopped fresh Italian flatleaf parsley

1   Put the Beaujolais and shallots in a heavy saucepan and bring to a boil. Reduce by two-thirds.

2   Add the game stock *(or beef stock)* to the wine mixture. Continue to simmer the sauce to reduce it again by half. Stir in the buerre manie and cook until the sauce thickens. Season to taste with salt and pepper; cover and keep warm.

3   In a skillet large enough to hold the 4 saddles of hare, heat the butter and canola oil over medium-high heat. Season the meat with salt and pepper, then place it in the skillet and sear it on all sides. For medium-rare, cook a total of about 5 to 7 minutes.

4   Remove the meat from the skillet and let cool slightly. Warm a serving platter.

5   With the point of a sharp knife, carve the meat from the bone, leaving each boned saddle of meat intact. Arrange the meat on the warm platter.

6   Reheat the Beaujolais sauce and add the tarragon and parsley. Stir.

7   To serve, pour the Beaujolais sauce generously over the meat.

Grilled Loin of Mountain Sheep in Vodka Marinade

Serves 4

Mountain sheep or goat meat is flavorful but benefits from 48 hours in this vodka-based marinade that ensures a tender cut. The final flambé step is not absolutely necessary to finish the dish but certainly adds a dramatic touch to the start of a meal!

4 boneless loins of mountain sheep, about 8 ounces each
(substitute mutton, moose, or chamois)
1 cup vodka, plus additional for flaming (about 2 tablespoons)
juice of 1 lemon
1 tablespoon chopped fresh thyme leaves
1 bay leaf
⅔ cup canola oil
salt and freshly ground pepper

1   Place the meat in a container just large enough to hold it tightly, or use a zip-lock plastic storage bag.

2   Whisk together the vodka, lemon juice, thyme, bay leaf, and oil. Pour the marinade over the meat; seal and refrigerate for 48 hours.

3   Prepare coals for outdoor grilling. Drain the meat from the marinade (discard the marinade), season with salt and pepper, and let rest for 15 minutes. When the grill is hot, sear the meat for 5 minutes on each side for medium-rare, 2 to 3 minutes longer per side for medium.

4   When the meat is cooked to the desired degree of doneness, place the loins on a flameproof platter, spoon on fresh vodka, and carefully ignite with a long match. The vodka will burn off rapidly. Serve immediately with a side dish of couscous or rice.

Ostrich Tenderloin
au Poivre

SERVES 4 AS A MAIN COURSE

¼ cup black peppercorns

1 whole tenderloin of ostrich, about 2 pounds

(substitute tenderloin of venison, buffalo, or beef)

¼ teaspoon salt

3 tablespoons canola oil

3 tablespoons unsalted butter

2 small stalks celery, minced

1 medium onion, minced

2 teaspoons all-purpose flour

2 plum tomatoes, peeled, seeded, and diced

1 bouquet garni *(see page 3)*

2 cups water

1 cup dry white wine

1 large sprig fresh tarragon

salt and freshly ground pepper

1 cup port

1 teaspoon heavy cream

1 teaspoon brandy

1 tablespoon Italian flatleaf parsley, chopped

1 Coarsely crush the peppercorns using a rolling pin or a mortar and pestle. Season the tenderloin with the salt, then roll it in the crushed peppercorns to coat evenly, gently pressing the pepper into the meat. Set aside.

2 In a sauté pan, heat 1 tablespoon each of canola oil and butter. Add the celery and onion and cook until golden, 10 to 12 minutes. Sprinkle the flour over the vegetables and stir well. Add the tomatoes, bouquet garni, water, and wine. Cover and simmer over low heat for 45 minutes. Add the tarragon sprig and simmer another 15 minutes.

3 Uncover and continue to simmer until the sauce thickens. Remove the bouquet garni and tarragon sprig. Puree the sauce in a blender or food processor and return it to the pan. Season to taste with salt and pepper and keep hot.

4 Preheat oven to 350°F. Warm a serving platter. In an ovenproof skillet large enough to hold the tenderloin, heat the remaining 2 tablespoons of oil, plus 1 tablespoon of butter. When hot, sear the tenderloin on all sides, a total of 5 minutes for medium-rare, 2 to 3 minutes longer for medium. Quickly place the pan in the preheated oven and roast, basting often, for an additional 12 minutes for medium-rare (15 minutes for medium).

5 Transfer the tenderloin to the warm serving platter and drain the excess fat from the pan. Deglaze the pan with the port, and simmer until reduced by half. Add the tomato-wine sauce, cream, and brandy. Bring to a boil and whisk in the remaining tablespoon of butter.

6 Slice the tenderloin into ½-inch-thick medallions, arrange on the platter and pour the sauce evenly over the meat. Garnish with the chopped parsley.

READYING MEATS AND FISH FOR COOKING

Chef Blondin always removes meats and thick fish fillets from the refrigerator at least 20 minutes before they are to be cooked—a simple trick that brings the meat up in temperature so that it will cook more evenly in the oven, in a skillet, or on the grill.

TOMATOES WITH HERBED GAME MEAT STUFFING

MAKES 4 SERVINGS

A great way to use leftover roasted game meats of any type.

4 fresh large tomatoes, ripe but firm
1 pound game meat leftovers
½ pound pork shoulder
5 ounces chicken livers
1 tablespoon fresh tarragon, chopped
1 tablespoon very finely chopped fresh rosemary leaves
1 tablespoon chopped fresh cilantro
1 tablespoon chopped fresh parsley
1 whole egg
1 ounce brandy
salt and freshly ground black pepper to taste

1   Preheat the oven to 350°F.

2   Carefully carve off the tomato tops and reserve them. With a soup spoon scoop out the seeds and pulp from the tomatoes. Lightly salt the cavities.

3   Grind the game meat together with the pork and chicken livers.

4   Combine the ground meat with the herbs, the egg, and the brandy. Season with salt and fresh pepper.

5   Divide the stuffing evenly to fill the tomatoes. Place them in a greased, ovenproof skillet or baking dish just large enough to hold the tomatoes, and replace the tops.

6   Bake for 30 minutes and serve from the dish at the table with a hearty grain accompaniment such as rice, barley, or couscous.

Tarragon Pot-Roasted Teal

Serves 4

*Potent and strongly aromatic, fresh French tarragon is the key
to enhancing the natural flavor of these succulent small wild ducks. Happily,
it's widely available throughout the U.S. You'll know the genuine article by its green,
herbaceous fragrance. Says Chef Blondin, it should "hit the nose immediately."*

10 sprigs freshest French tarragon
4 fresh teal, about 10 to 12 ounces each
(substitute Cornish game hen, or free-range chicken, quartered)
1 tablespoon soy sauce
1 tablespoon best-quality olive oil
2 shallots, finely chopped
5 tablespoons dry vermouth
salt and freshly ground black pepper to taste

1   Strip the leaves from the tarragon sprigs and reserve. Break the stems into small
pieces to release the fragrance and place inside the cavities of the birds. Truss the
legs and rub each bird all over with the soy sauce. Set aside for 30 minutes.

"I must confess that this is my favorite recipe in
The Hunter's Table. I've made it with duck and with game hens
and served it with tender potato dumplings drenched in the
delicious sauce that results from the slow simmering of birds in
dry vermouth. It's a splendid main course for a dinner party—a
rustic but elegant dish that fills the house with the most amaz-
ing aroma. I cook it in my big black cast iron casserole, bring
the whole pot to the table and raise the lid for a bit of drama
when the dinner is ready."

—Terry Libby

2   Preheat the oven to 350°F. Heat the olive oil in an ovenproof skillet or Dutch oven just large enough to hold all four birds. Fry the shallots in the ovenproof skillet or Dutch oven until soft, but do not brown.

3   Place the teal in the ovenproof skillet or Dutch oven with the shallots. Cook, turning often, until the birds are evenly browned on all sides. Add the vermouth and all but one generous tablespoon of the tarragon leaves to the pan. (Reserve the tablespoon of tarragon for a final garnish.)

4   Bring to a gentle simmer, cover the pan, and transfer to the oven. Bake for approximately 25 minutes, depending on the size of the birds: slightly less time for very small teal, or 5 to 10 minutes additional cooking time for plumper birds.

5   Remove the casserole from the oven and arrange the teal on a serving platter. Strain the pan juices over the birds and season lightly with salt and pepper. Garnish with the reserved tarragon leaves.

Creamy Gratin of Duck Breast and Rice

Serves 4

*A dish of tender duck breasts poached in milk and topped
with nutty Gruyère cheese is the richest of comfort foods on a chilly night.
Pair with a bold Chardonnay or a light red wine.*

8 wild duck breasts, skinless and boneless, about 1½ pounds total
(substitute breast of chicken, turkey, or farm-raised duck)
2 cups whole milk
5 tablespoons unsalted butter
2 tablespoons flour
¼ cup heavy cream
salt and freshly ground pepper to taste
3 cups hot cooked rice, best if prepared "Créole" Style *(see page 119)*
¼ cup grated Gruyère, or other imported Swiss cheese

1   Soak the duck breasts in the cold milk for 1 hour (covered and refrigerated).

2   Drain the milk into a heavy saucepan large enough to hold the duck. Bring to a boil
and add the duck breasts. Lower the heat to a gentle simmer and poach the meat for
8 minutes. Drain the milk from the pan and reserve. Place the duck breasts on a
platter and cover to keep warm.

3   Melt 3 tablespoons of butter in the saucepan. Add the flour and cook, stirring
constantly over medium heat to make a lightly golden roux. Gradually add in the
reserved hot milk and continue to stir over medium heat until the sauce is smooth
and thickened.

4   Stir in the cream and continue to simmer until the sauce is reduced by about one-
third. Season to taste with salt and pepper.

5   Prepare the rice and keep hot. Preheat the oven to 425°F. Butter a shallow baking
dish or au gratin dish.

6   To assemble the dish, first spread the cooked rice evenly in the baking pan. Arrange
the duck breasts on top of the rice and pour the warm cream sauce over the dish.
Sprinkle with the grated cheese and dot with the remaining 2 tablespoons of butter.

7   Bake until hot and bubbly and the top is well browned.

Duck Legs Baked "Miroton" Style

Serves 4

*"Miroton" is a country French preparation combining the flavors
of sweet cooked onions and tart pickles. It is usually made with beef,
but duck leg quarters work equally well. Serve with* Hunter Potatoes
Lyonnaise *(see page 103) or* Potatoes Fondant *(see page 107).*

2 tablespoons olive oil

3 tablespoons unsalted butter

2 large white onions, peeled and diced

1 cup French cornichons (tiny vinegar pickles)**, coarsely chopped**

½ cup red wine vinegar

1 tablespoon tomato paste

4 duck leg quarters, about 8 ounces each

(substitute 2 pounds beef top round)

salt and freshly ground pepper to taste

½ cup grated Gruyère cheese

1   Preheat the oven to 350°F. Butter a shallow 2-quart baking dish or au gratin pan.

2   Heat the oil and butter together in a skillet. Add the onions, ¾ cup of the chopped pickles, the vinegar, and the tomato paste, and stir to combine. Bring to a boil and cook over high heat for 3 minutes.

3   Season the duck leg quarters with salt and pepper and arrange them in a single layer in the baking dish. Pour the warm onion and pickle mixture evenly over the duck, then sprinkle with the grated cheese and remaining ¼ cup chopped pickles. Cover loosely with foil and bake for 25 minutes, then remove the foil and bake uncovered for an additional 15 minutes or until the top is golden brown.

For Beef "Miroton": Cook as directed above, but allow for 1 hour total baking time (45 minutes covered; 15 minutes uncovered).

Honey-Grilled Goose Breast

Serves 4 to 6

2 whole goose breasts, about 1 pound each
(substitute large Muscovy duck breasts,
young turkey breast, or whole ostrich tenderloin)

salt and freshly ground pepper to taste
½ cup unsalted butter, very soft
3 tablespoons Dijon mustard
½ cup honey
1 teaspoon finely chopped fresh rosemary leaves

1 Season the meat on all sides with salt and pepper. Cover, set aside, and bring to room temperature.

2 In a bowl combine the soft butter, mustard, honey, and rosemary. Coat the goose breasts with the honey-mustard mixture and seal in a ziplock plastic bag. Set aside for 2 hours prior to grilling, "massaging" the bag every 20 minutes to ensure that the goose breast absorbs the honey-mustard flavors. (Do not refrigerate, but keep in a cool area.)

3 Prepare a charcoal grill or heat a range-top grill to medium heat. Remove the breasts from the bag and scrape off and reserve the honey-mustard mixture in a separate bowl.

4 Cook the goose breasts, turning and basting frequently with the reserved honey-mustard mixture. Total grilling time should be 25 to 35 minutes, depending on the thickness of the breasts. Transfer to a serving platter and let rest for 10 minutes. Slice and serve.

> "What is sauce for the goose may be sauce for the gander,
> but it is not necessarily sauce for the chicken, the duck,
> the turkey, or the Guinea hen."
> —Alice B. Toklas

Breast of Wild Goose in Ginger-Curry Sauce

½ cup plus 3 tablespoons unsalted butter

3 medium yellow onions, minced

2 teaspoons curry powder

2 cups Chicken Stock (*see page 16;* if canned, use unsalted)

1 Granny Smith apple, peeled, cored, and coarsely chopped

1 clove garlic, minced

1 bouquet garni (*see page 3*)

salt and freshly ground black pepper

½ cup heavy cream

juice of ½ lemon, freshly squeezed

2 tablespoons peeled and minced fresh ginger

1 whole boneless, skinless goose breast, about 2 pounds

(substitute turkey, capon, duck, or chicken)

2 tablespoons canola oil

2 tablespoons fresh chives, chopped

1 Melt the ½ cup butter in a skillet over medium heat. Add the onions and cook until soft and golden brown, about 15 minutes.

2 Add the curry powder, stir, and cook for 2 minutes longer.

3 Add the stock, chopped apple, garlic, and bouquet garni. Season lightly with salt and fresh pepper. Simmer, covered, over low heat for 45 minutes.

4 Strain the sauce through a fine wire mesh or chinois into a heavy saucepan. Add the cream, lemon juice, and ginger. Add additional salt and pepper to taste.

5 Cut the goose breast into 4 equal strips, lengthwise. Heat the oil and the 3 tablespoons of butter in another large skillet. Brown the goose breast fillets on all sides until golden. Season lightly with salt and fresh pepper. Cover the pan and cook over low heat for an additional 15 minutes.

6 Reheat the curry-ginger sauce. Place the goose breasts on a serving platter and pour the hot sauce over them. Garnish with the fresh chopped chives and serve with aromatic basmati rice or simple steamed potatoes.

Casserole of Pickled Goose Leg in Champagne Vinegar

Serves 4 as a main course

A tangy main dish for a casual lunch or dinner.

2 whole legs of goose
(substitute turkey leg, pork, or beef)
salt and freshly ground pepper
3 small white onions, sliced (about one cup)
3 plum tomatoes, peeled, seeded and diced
1 cup dry white wine
2 tablespoons canola oil
3 tablespoons unsalted butter
1 cup chopped French cornichons (tiny vinegar pickles)
1 tablespoon tomato puree
½ cup Champagne vinegar
½ cup grated Swiss cheese, such as Gruyère or Emmenthaler

1   Lightly oil a skillet and place over medium heat. Season the goose legs with salt and pepper and sear in the skillet until brown on all sides. Add ⅓ cup of the onion, the tomatoes, and the wine. Reduce heat, cover, and simmer for about 45 minutes. Remove from the heat and set aside until cool enough to handle.

2   In another skillet, heat the canola oil and butter. Add the remaining onions, ¾ cup chopped pickles, tomato puree, and the vinegar. Cook over high heat for 3 minutes. Set aside.

3   Butter a shallow, broilerproof baking dish and preheat the broiler. Pull the goose meat from the bones, discarding bones and skin. Slice the meat and arrange it in the bottom of the broiling dish.

4   Place the remaining chopped pickles over the meat and top with the onion, pickle, and tomato mixture. Sprinkle with the cheese and broil until the top is brown and bubbling. Serve from the casserole at the table, along with a crusty loaf of bread and a green salad.

STEAMED BREAST OF GUINEA HEN WITH ESSENCE OF TRUFFLE

SERVES 4

Medallions of delicate guinea hen are stuffed with BELL PEPPER RAGOÛT
(see page 117) and served over piping hot SOUBISE SAUCE, *(see page 139)*
rich with sweet onions and butter. A final spoonful of essence of truffle oil
makes this a most elegant presentation. Serve with your finest Chardonnay.

4 breasts of guinea hen (about 2 pounds), boneless and skinless
(substitute pheasant or chicken breasts)
salt and freshly ground pepper to taste
2 teaspoons fresh, chopped Italian flatleaf parsley
3 tablespoons BELL PEPPER RAGOÛT *(see page 117)*
4 teaspoons white truffle oil
SOUBISE SAUCE *(see page 139)*

good kitchen twine

1   Place the guinea hen breasts on a cutting board and, using your fingers, gently pull away the long narrow strip of tenderloin and set aside. Using the sharp tip of a knife, make a deep butterfly cut lengthwise through each breast. Lay each open and flat on the cutting board and place a reserved tenderloin strip in the center of each breast. Lightly season the inside of each breast with salt and pepper and sprinkle with parsley.

2   Place a few strips of BELL PEPPER RAGOÛT across the narrow end of each breast. Then, starting at the narrow tip of the breast meat, carefully roll the breast into a tight cylinder shape. Enclose each breast in a generous length of plastic wrap, rolling it on the cutting board to press out any air pockets. Secure the ends by twisting the plastic wrap and tying with kitchen twine.

3   To cook, gently transfer the cylinders to a large pan of gently simmering water and cook for 12 to 15 minutes. Remove the cylinders from the pan, taking care not to puncture the plastic wrap. Set the cylinders aside until cool enough to handle, about 10 minutes.

4   To serve, remove the plastic wrap and slice each breast into several ¾-inch medallions. Arrange on a serving platter, or on individual plates, in a pool of buttery SOUBISE SAUCE. Drizzle each serving with approximately 1 teaspoon of truffle oil.

GRILLED PARTRIDGES

SERVES 4

Use any mustard you prefer in this recipe, such as a tarragon or a green peppercorn Dijon. If you can find it, use the rare French purple mustard, "mout de raisin" made with the tangy sediments collected from barrels of red wine. It imparts deep flavor and a burgundy color to the meat. Serve the partridges with chilled FRENCH POTATO SALAD *(see page 50).*

2 partridges, 1 to 1½ pounds each, halved
(substitute hen pheasants, pigeons, Cornish game hens, or poussins [baby chickens])
½ cup olive oil
4 teaspoons balsamic vinegar
¼ cup Dijon mustard
1 teaspoon chopped fresh thyme leaves
1 teaspoon chopped fresh cilantro
salt and freshly ground pepper to taste
1 tablespoon chopped fresh Italian flatleaf parsley

1   Trim the backbones from the partridges and remove the skin. In a bowl, mix together the olive oil, vinegar, mustard, thyme, and cilantro. Season lightly with salt and pepper.

2   Place the partridges in a zip-lock storage bag large enough to hold them tightly. Add the mustard mixture to the bag and toss to ensure that the meat is thoroughly coated.

3   Let the meat marinate for 2½ hours at room temperature. Gently "massage" the bags every 20 minutes or so to be sure that the meat absorbs the flavors of the marinade.

4   Meanwhile, prepare a charcoal grill, or heat a range-top grill to medium-hot. Remove the partridges from the bags and shake off the excess marinade. Place them on the grill and cook 15 to 20 minutes, turning frequently so that the meat is evenly cooked.

5   When the partridges are crisp and brown and the juices run clear from the thigh, serve immediately, garnished with chopped parsley and a side of chilled FRENCH POTATO SALAD *(see page 50).*

THE HUNTER'S TABLE

"Describe the perfect menu for a game-bird dinner," I asked Chef Blondin.

"You must have first a hot, then a cold appetizer," he replied. After some thought he offered this plan, in this order:

Brandied Duck Liver Pâté

Tart of Wild Leeks in Custard

Grilled Partridge with Pan-Fried Corn Cakes

Hazelnut-Endive Salad with Goat Cheese

Warm Apple Tart with Fresh Rosemary

"And which wine would you choose?" I asked.

Blondin was silent for a full two minutes.

"We have the partridge, the duck, the leeks. So… we'll do a red zinfandel with this."

Leg of Guinea Hen
en Croûte

Serves 4

*Roasting a leg of guinea hen in puff pastry makes an
impressive main course and is by no means as difficult as it looks.
Serve with* POTATOES FONDANTE *(see page 107) and*
RED CURRANT SAUCE FOR GAME *(see page 135).*

4 guinea hen leg quarters with skin, about 8 ounces each
(substitute duck, pheasant, or chicken)
salt and fresh ground pepper
1 tablespoon canola oil
1 tablespoon unsalted butter
4 ounces puff pastry (ready-made frozen puff pastry is fine)
½ cup prepared MUSHROOM DUXELLE *(see page 126)*
for an egg wash: 1 egg beaten with 1 teaspoon heavy cream

1   Partially bone each leg quarter by removing the thigh bone, leaving the drumstick bone intact. Season lightly with salt and pepper.

2   Heat the oil and butter in a heavy skillet. Brown each leg quarter on all sides, 8 to 10 minutes. Transfer to a platter and cover loosely.

3   Preheat the oven to 350°F and line a baking sheet with waxed or parchment paper.

4   Roll out the puff pastry to make four 6x6-inch squares. Place a leg quarter, skin-side down, on each pastry square. Stuff 2 tablespoons of the Mushroom Duxelles mixture into each thigh, making a small additional slit in the meat if necessary. Brush the edges of the pastry square with water, then fold the pastry around the leg quarter to encase it completely, leaving just the tip of the drumstick bone exposed. Be sure to leave no air pockets and to seal the dough over the Mushroom Duxelles.

5   Quickly flip the leg quarters over and onto the baking sheet, seam-side down. Using a fine pastry brush, glaze each with egg wash. Arrange decorative pastry leaf cut-outs on top and brush again with egg wash. Bake for 20 minutes or until the pastry is light golden brown. Serve hot from the oven.

CHARDONNAY-ROASTED PHEASANT
WITH ARTICHOKE HEARTS

SERVES 4 TO 6 AS A MAIN COURSE

*Fresh artichokes are by far the best choice for use in this dish, but the marinated type,
well-drained of all oil and seasonings will do nicely. A hearty barley-rice pilaf or
TENDER POTATO DUMPLINGS (see page 108) would make the perfect accompaniment.*

¼ cup walnut oil
Two 2-pound pheasants, quartered
(substitute free-range chicken or guinea hen)
salt and freshly ground pepper to taste
10 whole shallots, peeled
3 large cloves fresh garlic, minced
1 cup good-quality Chardonnay
2 tablespoons unsalted butter
12 artichoke hearts
2 tablespoons chopped fresh tarragon leaves

1   Preheat the oven to 350°F.

2   Heat the walnut oil in a heavy, ovenproof skillet large enough to hold all the
     pheasant quarters.

3   Season the pheasant lightly with salt and pepper. When the skillet is hot, place the
     pheasant pieces, skin-side down in the pan. Cook without turning until golden
     brown, then turn carefully to brown on both sides.

4   Cover the skillet and place in the preheated oven for 15 minutes.

5   Return the skillet to the stove-top. Add the whole shallots and minced garlic and
     sauté over low heat for 2 minutes, stirring gently to keep the browned pheasant skins
     intact. Deglaze with the Chardonnay and remove the skillet from the heat.

6   In a separate sauté pan, melt the butter over medium heat. Add the artichoke hearts,
     season with salt and pepper, and sauté for 5 minutes. Pour the artichokes and butter
     evenly over the pheasant, cover the skillet, and return it to the oven for an additional
     10 minutes.

7   To serve, place 1 or 2 pheasant pieces in the center of the plate, surrounded by the
     roasted shallots and artichoke hearts. Pour pan juices over pheasant and garnish
     with the fresh chopped tarragon.

PHEASANT BAKED IN A SALT CRUST

SERVES 4 AS A MAIN COURSE

Roasting a whole pheasant—or any bird—encased inside a salt crust will
season the meat as it bakes, and seal in the juices. There's no special trick
to this technique. Place a carved quarter of juicy pheasant over a serving
of hot HUNTER POTATOES WITH WILD MUSHROOMS *(see page*
103) and drizzle with RED CURRANT SAUCE FOR GAME *(see page 135).*
Use the hand-harvested sea salt from Normandy called "Sels de fleurs"
for a truly French touch. The salt is very coarse, slightly damp,
and gray in color. It is sold in gourmet and specialty markets.

1 pheasant, 3–4 pounds
(substitute a small duck or free-range chicken)
Salt and freshly ground pepper to taste
3½ cups all-purpose flour
1 cup water
½ cup regular table salt
1 cup sea salt, imported *Sels de fleurs* **if available**
1 egg white
2 tablespoons RENDERED DUCK FAT *(see page 140)***, or canola oil**
1 whole egg, beaten

1   Preheat the oven to 350°F. Rinse the pheasant thoroughly and pat dry. Season lightly
    with salt and pepper inside and out. Truss the bird.

2   In a large mixing bowl combine the flour, water, and the ½ cup table salt. Mix well to
    make a stiff dough. Add the sea salt and the egg white. Cover the bowl with a damp
    towel and refrigerate.

3   In a large, heavy skillet, heat the duck fat until very hot. Sear the whole pheasant,
    turning gently with tongs, until golden brown on all sides. Transfer to a platter to
    cool for at least 15 minutes.

4   Remove the dough from the refrigerator and, using your hands, press the dough over
    the pheasant to encrust it in a half-inch-thick coating all around, completely sealing
    the pheasant in the salt crust. Let rest for 10 minutes.

5   Place the pheasant on a baking sheet and brush the crust with the beaten egg. Bake
    for 50 minutes, a few minutes more for a larger bird. Remove from the oven and
    break away and discard the salt crust. Quarter the pheasant and serve while hot.

PITHIVIER OF HAZEL GROUSE (A GAME PIE)

MAKES 4 MAIN-COURSE SERVINGS

4 whole, cleaned, skinned grouse, about 1 pound each
(substitute wild duck, wood pigeon, or any small game bird)
salt and freshly ground pepper
2 teaspoons Cognac
1 ounce plus 2 teaspoons heavy cream
¼ cup chopped fresh Italian flatleaf parsley
1 tablespoon chopped fresh tarragon
1 sheet puff pastry (ready-made is fine)
1 egg yolk
1 cup RED CURRANT SAUCE FOR GAME *(see page 135)*

1   Remove the grouse meat from the bones. Reserving the breast meat, mince or coarsely grind the rest of the meat. Season the minced meat with salt and fresh pepper, then stir in the Cognac, 1 ounce of cream, the parsley, and tarragon. Cover and set aside.

2   On a lightly floured surface, roll out the puff pastry sheet to ⅛-inch thickness. Cut out four 5-inch rounds and four 6-inch rounds.

3   Preheat the oven to 350°F. Line a baking sheet with parchment paper. Place the 5-inch rounds of puff pastry on the sheet. Place one breast half on each pastry round. Divide the minced meat mixture into four equal portions and place them on top of the breast meat, then place the second breast half on top of the minced meat to make three layers. Cover with the remaining 6-inch pastry rounds, folding the edges under and pinching the dough to seal the pithiviers.

4   With the point of a sharp knife carve a small ¼-inch hole in the center of each pithivier to release steam while they bake. Beat the egg yolk with the 2 remaining teaspoons of cream to make an egg wash. Brush the mixture on lightly with a pastry brush.

5   Bake for 25 minutes until light golden brown. Serve hot with RED CURRANT SAUCE FOR GAME.

Poached Waterhen in Curry Suprême

Serves 4

1 fresh waterhen, about 3 pounds
(substitute free-range chicken)
salt and freshly ground black pepper to taste
2 very thin sheets pork fatback, about 5x5 inches square
3 quarts Rich Chicken Stock *(see page 16)*
2 tablespoons unsalted butter
¼ cup all-purpose flour
1 tablespoon curry powder
½ cup heavy cream
1 tablespoon chopped fresh Italian flatleaf parsley

good kitchen twine

1   Rinse the bird and pat dry. Season the cavity with salt and pepper. Wrap the fatback sheets around the bird and, using a few lengths of kitchen twine, tie the fatback on securely.

2   Transfer the waterhen to a large saucepan and add the stock to cover. Bring to a gentle boil, cover, and simmer for 1 hour. Every 10 to 15 minutes, remove the lid from the pan and skim the surface with a shallow spoon to remove excess foam and fat.

3   Remove the waterhen from the pot, draining any juices back into the stock; reserve the poaching liquid. Remove the fatback "wrapper," and place the waterhen on a serving platter. Cover it loosely with foil or a towel to keep it warm.

4   In a smaller saucepan, melt the butter. Add the flour and curry to make a seasoned roux, stirring the mixture constantly over low heat for 5 minutes. Add 2 cups of the poaching liquid, raise heat to medium-high, and whisk constantly until the sauce reaches a boil. Whisk in the cream and add salt and pepper to taste.

5   To serve, strain the hot sauce over the whole waterhen and garnish with the chopped parsley. Carve at table, spooning the sauce over each serving. Serve with a rice pilaf or pasta side dish.

BROILED PIGEONS
WITH SPICED CARAMELIZED ONIONS

SERVES 4 AS A MAIN COURSE

¼ cup unsalted butter

6 medium white onions, minced

salt and freshly ground black pepper to taste

2 pigeons, about 1 pound each, halved and partially boned

(substitute ptarmigans, ring doves, or Cornish game hens)

½ teaspoon ground cumin

¼ teaspoon ground ginger

¼ teaspoon curry powder

¼ teaspoon ground cinnamon

2 tablespoons freshly squeezed lemon juice

1　Heat the butter in a sauté pan. Add the onions and cook over medium heat for 45 minutes, stirring frequently until sweet and lightly browned (caramelized). Season to taste with salt and pepper.

2　To partially bone the pigeons, use a sharp carving or filleting knife. Lay the pigeon breast-side down on a cutting board. Butterfly by splitting the pigeon in half along the vertebrae. Slip the sharp point of the knife along the breast bone, carefully pulling it away from the pigeon, leaving the leg and thigh bone intact.

3　Blend the dry spices together in a small bowl and set aside. Set the broiler to high heat. Season the pigeons with salt and pepper on the cut side, leaving the skin unseasoned. Place them skin-side up in a shallow, broilerproof pan. Transfer the pan to the preheated broiler.

4　Broil the pigeons for about 12 minutes, or until the skins are brown and crisp. Remove the pan from the oven and sprinkle the spice mixture evenly over the skins. Pour any pan juices into the caramelized onions. Pour the lemon juice over the birds.

5　To serve, have ready 4 warm dinner plates. Make a bed of onions on each plate and place a half pigeon on top.

> "Whatever the reason, a roasted pigeon is and long has been the most heartening dish to set before a man bowed down with grief or loneliness."
>
> —MFK FISHER from *The Art of Eating*

Ptarmigan Breast with Red Peppers in Cardamom Marinade

Serves 4 as a light entrée

The ptarmigan is a rare Scottish game bird, often available only through specialty game suppliers, but the breast of any fowl will work in this recipe: partridge, squab, guinea hen, duck, or chicken. The meat will take on the tangy flavors of citrus and cardamom. For an elegant picnic, pack this dish along with French bread, a fine cheese, and a bottle of Merlot.

2 red bell peppers, roasted *(see below)*
2 tablespoons olive oil
2 tablespoons hazelnut oil
2 small onions, thinly sliced (about 1 cup)
3 carrots, peeled and cut into 1-inch julienne strips
1 cup dry white vermouth
juice of 1 lemon (at least 2 tablespoons)
1 bouquet garni *(see page 3)*
8 whole white peppercorns
8 fragrant green cardamom pods
salt and freshly ground pepper to taste
4 boneless, skinless breasts of ptarmigan, or other fowl (about 1 pound)
1 additional tablespoon olive oil to finish the dish

1   To roast the peppers: Preheat the broiler. Place the bell peppers in a shallow baking pan and place under the broiler. The skins will blacken as the peppers roast. Turn them frequently until they are roasted evenly on all sides, about 15 minutes. Remove the pan from the oven, place the hot peppers in a plastic storage bag, and seal. When the peppers are cool enough to handle, their skins will peel off easily. Trim and seed the peppers and cut them into ½-inch-thick strips.

2   Heat the oils together in a heavy skillet over medium heat. Cook the onions and carrots until they are soft and lightly golden.

3 Add the vermouth, roasted pepper strips, lemon juice, bouquet garni, peppercorns, and cardamom to the pan. Season lightly with salt. Simmer, uncovered, over low heat for 20 minutes, adding water a tablespoon at a time if necessary to maintain a thick sauce.

4 Place the ptarmigan breasts in a separate saucepan. Pour the hot sauce over the breasts to cover. Cover the pan and simmer over low heat for 12 minutes.

5 Remove the bouquet garni and transfer the mixture to a ceramic casserole deep enough to hold the breasts submerged in the sauce. Let cool completely, then chill a bit before serving. Finish with a final drizzle of olive oil.

A MEMORABLE WOODCOCK

"What is the finest game meal you ever ate?" I asked Chef Blondin. With reverence he described a perfectly roasted woodcock, bagged and cooked by his friend, Chef Gerard Antonin.

"It was very, very delicate. The bird was roasted whole—plucked, but not gutted—which is very often done in France. You eat the tender meat, the breast and legs, then split the cock open and eat the soft, warm innards and brains. It is important to cook the bird just to the right degree of doneness when it's eaten this way."

Sautéed Quail
with Lemon Sauce and Pine Nuts

*Marinating the birds in beer will tenderize the meat
and enhance the juices. Rice is a good partner to this tangy preparation.*

8 quail, 6 to 8 ounces each
(substitute Cornish game hen)
2 cups imported "blonde" beer
1 tablespoon chopped fresh thyme leaves
salt and freshly ground pepper
all-purpose flour for dredging
3 tablespoons unsalted butter
4 tablespoons olive oil
½ cup pine nuts
juice of one lemon, freshly squeezed
3 cloves garlic, minced
2 tablespoons minced fresh Italian flatleaf parsley
2 tablespoons chopped fresh chervil
fresh lemon slices for garnish

1   Rinse the quail thoroughly and place them in a deep bowl. Add the beer and thyme. Cover and refrigerate for 30 minutes.

2   Remove the quail from the beer marinade, drain, and dry them. Season the birds with salt and pepper, then dredge in flour on all sides, shaking off any excess.

3   Heat 2 tablespoons of butter and the olive oil in large skillet over high heat. Gently place the quail in the skillet and brown on all sides for about 6 minutes total. Turn gently to avoid breaking the delicate skins. Add additional olive oil if needed to prevent sticking. Remove the birds from the skillet and drain on paper towels. Transfer to a warm serving platter and cover loosely with foil.

4   In another skillet, sauté the pine nuts in the remaining tablespoon of butter until golden. Add the lemon juice, garlic, and parsley. Sauté the mixture gently for 3 minutes.

5   Pour the pine nut and lemon mixture over the warm quail. Garnish with chopped chervil and lemon slices.

CLASSIC PAN-FRIED TROUT
WITH PECAN BUTTER

SERVES 4

*Whether it's prepared over an open campfire along a rushing stream,
or at home on the range-top, nothing beats sweet, fresh trout. A simple side dish
of rice CRÉOLE style (see page 119) is the perfect accompaniment.*

4 whole, fresh trout
1 cup whole milk
1 cup flour
1½ cup unsalted butter
salt and freshly ground pepper
⅔ cups pecan halves
1 tablespoon chopped fresh tarragon leaves
lemon wedges for garnish

1   Trout should be gutted, with heads removed, and butterfly-cut to spread open for quick pan-searing. Rinse the trout well and towel dry. Place the milk and flour in separate shallow pans for dredging.

2   Melt 1 cup of butter in a large, heavy skillet over high heat, being careful not to burn the butter. Dip each trout in the milk, then dredge lightly in the flour and place it quickly in the hot skillet.

3   Fry the trout until golden brown on each side, turning once. Depending on size, the fish should be cooked through in 3 to 5 minutes. Place the trout on a warm platter and season lightly with salt and pepper.

4   Melt the remaining ½ cup butter in the skillet and add the pecans. Toss the pecans in the butter until they begin to brown. Pour the butter and pecans over the fish, then garnish with chopped tarragon and lemon wedges.

Herb-Grilled Gulf Shrimp

Serves 2 as a main course

Succulent and delicious, peel and eat shrimp, cooked simply in a foil wrap.
Serve hot grilled shrimp as an appetizer or main course.

1 pound fresh raw shrimp, unpeeled, heads trimmed
(substitute crawfish or langoustines)
1 tablespoon chopped fresh thyme leaves
2 teaspoons fresh garlic, minced
2 tablespoons extra virgin olive oil
salt and freshly ground pepper
Scratch-Made Tartar Sauce *(see page 137)*

1   Heat a charcoal or range-top grill to medium-high.

2   In a bowl, toss the shrimp with the thyme, garlic, and olive oil. Season with salt and pepper.

3   Cut a large sheet of foil and place the shrimp mixture in the center. Fold in the edges and pinch to seal the packet.

4   Place the packet on the hot grill and cook for 8 to 10 minutes, until the shrimp are hot and just cooked through. Place the packet on a serving platter and cut open. Serve with lemon wedges and Scratch-made Tartar Sauce *(see page 137)*.

A Summer Meal of Wild Fish and Seafood

Chilled Great Lakes Smelt in Champagne Vinegar
Hot Appetizer of Herb-Grilled Gulf Shrimp
Classic Pan-Fried Trout with Pecan Butter and Wild Mushroom Couscous
Salad of Freshly-Picked Greens with Sweet and Sour Maple Vinaigrettte
Brandied Sour Cherry Clafoutis

"For this I would start with a crisp, cold Chardonnay,
then move on to a Sancerre when the trout is served."

—Chef Blondin

CIDER-GRILLED GREAT LAKES SMELT

SERVES 2 AS A MAIN COURSE

Cider adds a sweet touch to the fish, and char-grilling adds a little smoke.
This recipe can also be done in a standard oven or broiler at 350°F.

16 or more fresh smelt, gutted and heads removed, about 1 pound total
(substitute small perch or trout)
1 cup apple cider
3 tablespoons sour cream
3 tablespoons whole grain prepared mustard
1 tablespoon Calvados, brandy, or Cognac
1 Granny Smith apple, peeled, cored, and finely diced
salt and freshly ground pepper to taste
3 tablespoons canola oil

1   Rinse the smelt, drain, and pat them dry on a kitchen towel.

2   Place the smelt in a shallow glass pan and pour the cider over the fish. Cover with plastic wrap and marinate, refrigerated, for 30 minutes.

3   Prepare hot coals in an outdoor grill: wait until the coals are very hot, with white ash around the edges.

4   In a small bowl combine the sour cream, prepared mustard, brandy, diced apple, and salt and pepper to taste.

5   Remove the fish from the cider; drain. Cut a sheet of aluminum foil for the grill large enough to hold all the smelt in a single layer. Drizzle the foil with the oil. Place the smelt on the foil and put a small spoonful of the apple mixture inside each fish.

6   Carefully transfer the foil to the grill. Cook the fish, turning once or twice until cooked through, 2 or 3 minutes per side for very small smelt, 5 minutes per side for larger fish.

> "The ancient Gauls liked fishing in rivers with rod and line,
> and angling is still a favourite leisure pursuit in France."
>
> —TOUSSAINT-SAMAT,
> FROM *HISTORY OF FOOD*

CHARDONNAY CRÈME SAUCE FOR PAN-SEARED FISH

8 MAIN-COURSE PORTIONS OF FISH

This rich reduction of fish stock, wine, and cream turns any type of game fish into an elegant meal. In France it is called "Sauce Bonne Femme"—"Good Wife Sauce." Sear any fish fillet in a hot skillet with a bit of butter and oil, then top with warm sauce.

2 cups good-quality Chardonnay
2 cups FISH STOCK *(see page 15)*
5 medium shallots, thinly sliced
10 button mushrooms, thinly sliced (about 1 cup)
2 cups heavy cream
salt and freshly ground white pepper to taste

FOR THE GARNISH:

1 small ripe plum tomato, peeled, seeded, and chopped
1 tablespoon chopped fresh Italian flatleaf parsley
2 additional small mushrooms, thinly sliced

1   In a heavy saucepan over medium heat, bring the wine and fish stock to a boil.

2   Add the sliced shallots and 1 cup sliced mushrooms. Simmer over low heat until the mixture is reduced by half.

3   Add the cream and continue to simmer gently to reduce the mixture until thickened—it should coat the back of a spoon.

4   Strain the sauce through a fine wire mesh strainer or chinois, pressing with the back of spoon or ladle to extract all the liquid from the shallots and mushrooms. Discard the vegetables. Season with salt and white pepper.

5   Spoon the warm sauce onto a platter with pan-seared or hot poached fish, garnished with chopped tomato, parsley, and mushroom slices.

A Repertoire of Side Dishes

[continued]

Hunter's Potatoes Lyonnaise with Wild Mushrooms and Black Bear Bacon

Serves 4

3 large Yukon Gold potatoes

2 tablespoons canola oil, or Rendered Duck Fat *(see page 140)*

1 medium yellow onion, Spanish or Vidalia, in ¼-inch-thick slices

1 cup fresh wild mushrooms, such as chanterelles, hedgehog, or oyster

3 ounces black bear bacon, coarsely chopped

(substitute wild boar bacon, or pork bacon)

1 tablespoon chopped fresh thyme leaves

salt and freshly ground black pepper to taste

1   Peel and slice the potatoes ¼ inch thick. Drop them into a large pot of cold, salted water. Cover and bring to a boil. Cook until tender but still firm, about ten minutes. Drain the potatoes and let them dry as the steam rises for at least 5 minutes.

2   Heat the oil or fat in a large, heavy skillet. Add the potatoes and sauté for 8 minutes. Then add onions and cook for an additional 4 minutes. Add the mushrooms and bacon and turn the heat to medium-high. Cook for 5 minutes more, or until the potatoes turn golden brown. Add the chopped thyme and toss once more.

3   Before serving, quickly drain the potatoes on paper towels to degrease. Serve very hot.

"Pray for peace and grace and spiritual food, for wisdom and guidance, for all these are good—but don't forget the potatoes."
—J. T. Pettee

Cabernet Stewed Red Potatoes

Serves 4

Potatoes simmered in wine take on a rich red color.
Serve this hearty dish with venison loin or Buffalo Brochettes *(see page 70).*

1 tablespoon kosher salt
2 pounds small redskin or Yukon Gold potatoes
750 ml bottle Cabernet Sauvignon
¼ cup unsalted butter or Rendered Duck Fat *(see page 140)*
2 ounces double-smoked bacon, diced
1 small white onion, diced
6 celery stalks, cut into 1-inch slices
2 tablespoons flour
1 bouquet garni *(see page 3)*
2 tablespoons chopped fresh Italian flatleaf parsley
salt and freshly ground pepper to taste

1   Dissolve the kosher salt in a large bowl of very cold water. Peel the potatoes, leaving them whole, and drop them into the salted water. Set aside.

2   Pour the wine into a saucepan and bring to a simmer. Meanwhile, heat the butter, or duck fat, in a large saucepan or Dutch oven and cook the bacon until it is transparent. Add the onion and celery to the bacon and cook until soft, about 5 minutes. Sprinkle the flour over the bacon and vegetables and stir. Pour in the hot wine.

3   Transfer the potatoes from the salt water to the simmering wine mixture. Add the bouquet garni, cover, and simmer over low heat for 20 to 30 minutes or until the potatoes are fork-tender.

4   To serve, remove the bouquet garni and season with salt and pepper to taste. Transfer the potatoes to a serving dish and sprinkle liberally with the chopped fresh parsley.

Garlic and Rosemary Mashed Potatoes

Serves 4

2 whole bulbs garlic
1 tablespoon olive oil
4 large Idaho potatoes (2 pounds)
½ cup heavy cream
¾ cup unsalted butter, cut into bits
½ teaspoon finely chopped fresh rosemary leaves
salt and freshly ground pepper

1   Preheat the oven to 350°F. Coat the whole bulbs of garlic with the olive oil and seal loosely in an aluminum foil packet. Bake for 1 hour.

2   When the garlic has cooled, cut the bulbs in half and squeeze out the soft cloves. Using a fork, mash the garlic into a paste. Set aside.

3   Peel and quarter the potatoes. Place them in a large pot of lightly salted cold water to cover. Bring the pot to a boil and cook the potatoes until fork-tender but still firm. When the potatoes are done, drain them very thoroughly.

4   Heat the cream but do not boil. While potatoes are still hot, pass them through a ricer or food mill into a large mixing bowl. Add the butter, rosemary, and 1 tablespoon of the reserved garlic paste. Whip the potatoes with an electric mixer, or vigorously with a spatula, while adding the warm cream by spoonfuls to reach the desired consistency. Season to taste with salt and pepper and additional garlic paste, if you like. Reheat prior to serving if needed. Serve piping hot.

Country French
Scalloped Potatoes

Serves 4

Substitute wild ramps (wild onions) for leeks,
if you can find them, in early spring.

1 tablespoon butter, soft
1 medium leek, or a small bunch wild ramp onions
pinch of salt
3 large Idaho potatoes
1 cup water
2 cups heavy cream
pinch of freshly ground nutmeg
1 tablespoon minced garlic
salt and freshly ground pepper to taste

1   Preheat the oven to 325°F. Use the butter to coat a wide, shallow baking dish or casserole large enough to hold all the potatoes.

2   Trim the leeks (or ramps) at both ends, leaving the white and 3 inches of green stalk. Cut the stalk lengthwise, then slice into ¾-inch pieces. Thoroughly rinse the chopped leek to remove any sand that may be lodged between the layers. Drain.

3   Bring a small saucepan of water to a full boil, then add the pinch of salt and the chopped leeks. Blanch for about 2 minutes. Drain the leeks in a colander and rinse with cold water. Drain again thoroughly and set aside.

4   Peel the potatoes and slice ⅛-inch thick. Season with salt and pepper.

5   In large skillet or Dutch oven, combine the cup of water, the cream, the nutmeg, and garlic. Bring just to a boil. Season to taste with salt and freshly ground pepper. Place half the sliced potatoes in the buttered baking dish, top with all the leeks, then layer on the rest of the potatoes. Slowly pour the hot cream mixture over the potatoes.

6   Bake for a total of 45 minutes or until golden brown on top. NOTE: After the first 25 minutes of baking time, firmly press the top of the potatoes with a fork or spatula so that they remain covered with the cream mixture until they are done. Serve hot, directly from the bubbling casserole.

POTATOES FONDANTE

SERVES 4

12 small Yukon Gold potatoes (about 2 pounds)
2 thick strips smoked bacon (boar bacon if available)
½ cup unsalted butter
4 cups RICH CHICKEN OR DUCK STOCK *(see page 16)*
salt and freshly ground pepper to taste

1   Preheat the oven to 400°F. Peel the potatoes and cut into ¼-inch-thick slices.

2   Layer the potatoes evenly in a shallow casserole or au gratin baking dish. Dot with butter.

3   Dice the bacon and place over the potatoes.

4   Season the stock to taste with salt and pepper and pour it over the potatoes, leaving about one quarter of the potatoes uncovered. Bake for about 1 hour, or until the top is well browned.

TENDER POTATO DUMPLINGS

SERVES 4

*These elegant, melt-in-your-mouth potato dumplings
are tossed with buttery croutons for a bit of crunch-a perfect
accompaniment for richly flavored meat or fowl.*

1½ pounds Idaho baking potatoes
1½ cups best-quality white bread cubes, trimmed of crusts
8 tablespoons unsalted butter, at room temperature
salt and freshly ground black pepper to taste
a pinch of nutmeg
1 whole egg, plus 1 egg yolk
3 tablespoons finely minced fresh chives or chopped Italian flatleaf parsley
1 cup all-purpose flour
1½–2 tablespoons grated Swiss cheese

1   Preheat oven to 400°F. Bake the potatoes until they are very tender (40 to 60 minutes). While the potatoes are baking, place the bread cubes on a baking sheet and toast in the oven until just golden (10 to 15 minutes).

2   Holding the hot potatoes with a cloth, halve them and scoop out the pulp. Discard the skins. Press the pulp through the fine disk of a food mill, or a potato ricer. Stir in 3 tablespoons of the butter, salt, pepper, and nutmeg. Blend well. Stir in the whole egg, then the yolk, and 2 tablespoons of the minced chives, (or parsley) reserving 1 tablespoon for a final garnish.

3   Gradually add the flour one-third cup at a time. Mix in the grated cheese.

4   Cover a flat work surface with an 18-inch length of waxed or parchment paper. Using two soup spoons, form oval dumplings from the mixture (about 20), placing them gently on the paper.

5   Bring a large pot of salted water to a full boil. Carefully drop the dumplings in the pot and quickly reduce the heat to a bare simmer. Cook for 10 to 12 minutes. Remove one dumpling from the pot with a slotted spoon and taste for doneness. The dumplings should be firm but very tender. With a skimmer or slotted spoon, carefully remove the dumplings from the pot and drain.

6   While the dumplings are cooking, melt the remaining 5 tablespoons of butter in a skillet and cook until the butter reaches a rich, golden brown. Remove from heat at once. Add the toasted bread cubes and toss well.

7   With a skimmer or slotted spoon, transfer the dumplings to a warmed shallow bowl or platter. Top with the crouton and butter mixture and sprinkle with the reserved chives. Serve immediately.

Pan-Fried Corn Cakes

Makes 8 to 10 three-inch corn cakes

*Like country griddle cakes, these make a great addition
to the hunter's table for breakfast, lunch, or dinner, and are a delicious
accompaniment to soups and stews. This batter can be fried in a
skillet in a bit of oil, or baked in a preheated waffle iron.*

1 cup fresh sweet corn, trimmed from the cob
½ cup whole milk
5 tablespoons unsalted butter
2 egg yolks
½ cup heavy cream
½ cup sliced scallions
¾ cup sifted all-purpose flour
1 egg white
salt and freshly ground pepper to taste

1   Combine the corn and the milk in a small saucepan. Bring to a simmer and cook
until the corn is tender. Set aside to cool.

2   In another pan, melt the butter and set aside to cool.

3   Whisk the egg yolks together in a small mixing bowl. Add the cream, scallions, the
cooked corn and milk, and the melted butter. Add the sifted flour and mix well.

4   In a separate bowl, beat the egg white until soft peaks form. Fold the egg white into
the corn cake batter and season to taste with salt and pepper.

5   Heat a lightly oiled heavy skillet. (When the skillet is hot enough, a drop of batter
will spatter a bit as it hits the pan.) Spoon the batter into the pan to make 3-inch
corn cakes. Flip the cakes once as they begin to brown around the edges. Serve hot.

WHOLE GRAIN
MUSTARD SPÄTZLE

SERVES 4 TO 6

1 ¾ cups flour

4 whole eggs

2 tablespoons prepared whole grain mustard

1 tablespoon heavy cream

salt and freshly ground black pepper to taste

2 teaspoons unsalted butter

2 teaspoons chopped fresh chives

1   Sift the flour into a large mixing bowl and blend in the eggs, mustard, cream, salt, and pepper.

2   Bring a large saucepan or stockpot of lightly salted water to a full boil. Set aside a shallow bowl or strainer lined with paper towels.

3   To make the spätzle, use a spätzle press, or simply press small spoonfuls of dough through the holes of a colander, to make round noodlelike bits about an inch long. Drop the spätzle directly into the pot from the press or colander. When the spätzle rises to the surface, it is done. Do not overcook the spätzle; it should be al dente. Quickly remove the spätzle from the pot with a slotted spoon or strainer and drain in the bowl lined with paper towels.

4   In a frying pan, heat the butter and sauté the spätzle until light golden brown. Season with salt and pepper and garnish with chives.

Butter-Browned Potato Gnocchi

Serves 4

These hearty little potato dumplings are the ultimate comfort food. They benefit from the sauce or pan juices served with any game meat and make a magnificent meal in and of themselves when made with fine truffle oil and garnished with chopped fresh herbs. Serve them simply steamed, or sauté the finished gnocchi in a bit of butter until light golden brown.

3 large Idaho potatoes
½ cup flour
2 tablespoons white truffle oil
or 2 tablespoons extra virgin olive oil
½ teaspoon black truffle shavings (optional)
salt and freshly ground pepper to taste
3 tablespoons unsalted butter

1   Bake the potatoes in a 350°F oven until fork-tender, about 45 minutes.

2   When cool enough to handle, cut the potatoes in half and, using a large spoon, scoop the potato from the skins into a mixing bowl. Discard the skins.

3   Pass the potatoes through a ricer or the fine blade of a food mill. Sift the flour over the potatoes, add the oil and shaved truffles (if available), season with salt and pepper, and mix thoroughly.

4   Bring a large pot of lightly salted water to a light boil.

5   Divide the dough into 3 equal parts. On a floured work surface, roll each part into a long rope about 1 inch in diameter. Cut the ropes into ½-inch slices. To form each gnocchi, place a slice of dough on the tines of a fork, then press your finger into the dough to roll the gnocchi along the tines. The fork will leave ridges on the rounded outer surface of the gnocchi to give it added texture.

6   When all the gnocchi are formed, transfer them to the simmering water. Cook for just 1 or 2 minutes after the gnocchi rise to the surface. (Sample a dumpling to test for doneness.) When cooked through, drain the gnocchi immediately. Serve them simply boiled, tossed with a bit of butter, or proceed to the next step.

7   Heat the butter in a heavy skillet, add the drained gnocchi, and toss gently till golden brown, 7 to 10 minutes.

BAKED RIGATONI
WITH BASIL-TOMATO CREAM

SERVES 4

A rich side dish for roasted or grilled game birds or poultry.

8 ounces rigatoni
1 bunch fresh basil leaves, cut into fine strips (about 2 to 3 tablespoons)
½ cup diced plum tomatoes, peeled and seeded
1½ cup warm CLASSIC BÉCHAMEL SAUCE *(see page 141)*
1 teaspoon minced garlic
2 tablespoons grated Gruyère cheese

1   Preheat oven to 350°F. Have ready a 2-quart ovenproof casserole or au gratin dish.

2   Bring a large pot of salted water to a full boil. Cook the pasta until it is al dente, about 7 to 8 minutes. Drain well.

3   In a large bowl, toss the pasta with the basil, tomatoes, béchamel sauce, and garlic. Season to taste with salt and pepper. Transfer the mixture to the casserole and top with the grated cheese. Bake for 12 to 15 minutes, or until the cheese is brown and bubbly.

Water Rail Quenelles in Mushroom-Madeira Cream Sauce

Serves 4

Quenelles are delicate poached forcemeat dumplings, a French bistro classic. The quenelle mixture can be made in advance (covered and refrigerated), shaped into dumplings and cooked just before dinnertime—a recipe no more intimidating than any dumpling dish. Serve with a crusty bread and Country Herb Roquefort Butter *(see page 132).*

1 pound fresh water rail meat, boneless and skinless
(substitute hare, venison, or chicken)
2 shallots, minced
2 garlic cloves, minced
2 whole eggs
2 tablespoons flour, plus a bit extra for dredging
salt and freshly ground pepper to taste
2 tablespoons unsalted butter
1½ cups large domestic button mushrooms, sliced
2 egg yolks
½ cup heavy cream
2 tablespoons Madeira

1   Grind the water rail meat through the finest blade of a meat grinder. Stir the ground meat thoroughly with the shallots, garlic, whole eggs, and 1 tablespoon of the flour. Season lightly with salt and pepper and blend until the mixture is smooth.

2   Bring a large pot of salted water to a bare simmer. Lightly oil a large sheet of waxed or parchment paper, dust with flour, and lay it flat. Using 2 soup spoons, form oval dumplings from the mixture (about 20), placing them gently on the paper.

3   Cook one individual quenelle to test the consistency of the mixture. The quenelle should hold together while it cooks and should be very tender when done. If necessary, add an additional tablespoon or two of flour to the meat mixture to bind the quenelles.

4   When the mixture is right, dredge the quenelles lightly in additional flour and drop them into the hot salted water. Simmer very gently for 3 to 5 minutes, until hot completely through, then remove them with a slotted spoon and drain the quenelles on a towel. Reserve 1 cup of cooking liquid.

5   Heat the butter in a skillet over medium heat. Sauté the mushrooms until they begin to brown. Sprinkle 1 tablespoon of flour over them and toss thoroughly. Stir in the reserved cup of cooking liquid and carefully place the quenelles in the skillet. Let simmer, uncovered, over low heat for 5 minutes.

6   Transfer the hot quenelles to a heated serving dish. Beat the egg yolks with the cream and Madeira. Whisk the egg and cream mixture into the skillet and cook, stirring constantly, over very low heat until the sauce begins to thicken, about 2 to 3 minutes (do not boil). Pour the cream sauce over the hot quenelles and serve immediately.

Roasted Portobello Mushrooms

Serves 4

*These meaty mushrooms make a great addition
to any plate of grilled or roasted game meat.*

4 large portobello mushrooms
4 medium shallots, minced
½ cup balsamic vinegar
1½ cups olive oil
salt and freshly ground pepper to taste
1 generous tablespoon chopped, fresh chives

1 Using your fingers, peel the thin layer of skin from the tops of the mushroom caps. Trim the stems and brush the mushrooms clean.

2 Place the mushroom caps upside down in a shallow baking dish lined with waxed or parchment paper. Sprinkle the minced shallots over the mushrooms.

3 In a small mixing bowl, whisk together the vinegar and olive oil. Season to taste with salt and pepper. Pour the mixture over the mushroom caps, coating each one thoroughly. Allow the mushrooms to marinate at room temperature for at least 20 minutes.

4 Preheat the oven to 350°F. Bake the mushrooms uncovered, in the marinade, for 20 minutes. To serve, lift the mushrooms from the marinade, shaking off the excess, and serve garnished with chopped chives.

BELL PEPPER RAGOÛT

MAKES 2 CUPS

*A spoonful of this sweet condiment adds color and flavor
to a platter of game meat or poultry.*

**3 medium bell peppers, red, yellow, or a combination
1 tablespoon extra virgin olive oil
1 tablespoon unsalted butter
1 small white onion, thinly sliced
salt and freshly ground white pepper**

1   To roast the peppers: Preheat the broiler to medium-high. Rub the peppers evenly
    with the olive oil. Place them on a baking sheet and broil, just a few inches from the
    flame, turning frequently with tongs so that the skin is blistered on all sides,
    10 to 15 minutes.

2   Place the hot peppers in a deep bowl and cover immediately with plastic wrap.
    The steam from the hot peppers will continue to cook them and, once cooled, the
    skins will peel off easily.

3   Meanwhile, heat the butter in a heavy saucepan and cook the sliced onion over
    medium heat until golden brown, 5 to 8 minutes.

4   Peel the peppers and remove the seeds. Slice them into long, narrow, ⅛-inch- wide
    strips.

5   Toss the pepper strips with the onion and season to taste with salt and white pepper.
    Serve warm or chilled.

Chestnut Stuffing
for Wild Turkey

Serves 6 (enough for a 5 to 7-pound bird)

This stuffing is a rich and meaty one, unlike standard bread-based versions.
Make it a day ahead to allow the flavors to develop —
it will do justice to the finest of birds.

¼ cup canola oil or Rendered Duck Fat *(see page 140)*
5 ounces fresh chicken livers
salt and freshly ground pepper to taste
10 ounces pork shoulder
1 clove garlic
1 medium onion
2 shallots
4 ounces fresh button mushrooms
2 whole eggs
¼ cup heavy cream
¼ cup fine bread crumbs
⅓ cup brandy
1 tablespoon chopped fresh Italian flatleaf parsley
1 tablespoon chopped fresh sage
10 ounces fresh chestnuts, cooked and peeled,
or good-quality canned chestnuts, coarsely chopped

1 Heat the oil (or rendered duck fat) in a sauté pan over medium-high heat.

2 Sauté the chicken livers for about two minutes — do not cook them through. Remove them from the skillet, set them aside in a small bowl to hold their juices, and season them lightly with salt and pepper.

3 Using a medium-coarse grinder, grind together the pork, garlic, onion, shallots, mushrooms, and reserved chicken liver.

4 In a large bowl, lightly beat the eggs and cream together. Add the bread crumbs, brandy, parsley, sage, chestnuts, and the ground meat mixture. Season again, lightly, with salt and pepper. The mixture is now ready for stuffing. Storing the mixture, well-covered, in the refrigerator for 24 hours prior to use will enhance the blend of flavors. Note: Always wait to stuff the bird just prior to roasting.

RICE COOKED "CRÉOLE" STYLE

SERVES 4

*The favored French Caribbean method for preparing basic white rice —
not to be confused with the spicy Louisiana version.*

1½ cups converted rice, uncooked, such as Uncle Ben's
3 tablespoons unsalted butter
salt and freshly ground pepper to taste

1   Preheat the oven to 325°F. Lightly butter a 2-quart casserole dish.

2   Rinse the rice in cold water and drain well in a fine strainer or colander.

3   Bring 5 cups of salted water to a full boil. Add the rice, return the pot to a boil, and simmer (parboil) for 12 minutes. Quickly drain the rice again, shaking off as much cooking liquid as possible.

4   Place the rice in the casserole and bake, uncovered, for 10 minutes. Dot with butter, season with salt and pepper, and mix well before serving.

CRISPY WILD RICE

SERVES 4

*A simple cooking technique is all that's needed to
enhance the full, earthy flavor of wild rice.*

5 cups CHICKEN OR DUCK STOCK *(see page 16)*
1 cup wild rice
1 tablespoon unsalted butter
salt and freshly ground pepper to taste

1   In a heavy saucepan, bring the stock to a boil. Add the rice and cook until
the grains begin to open and the rice is tender but firm and still a bit chewy, about
45 minutes.

2   Drain the rice thoroughly in a colander or sieve. Melt the butter over medium heat in
a nonstick skillet, add the rice, and sauté until it is sizzling and slightly crispy, about
10 minutes. Season to taste with salt and pepper and serve.

NUTTED CITRUS PILAF
OF WILD RICE

SERVES 4 TO 6

Preparing this side dish an hour or two in advance allows the flavors to develop.
This autumn pilaf goes well with roasted duck, goose, or turkey.

CRISPY WILD RICE *(see previous page)*
1 cup pecan halves
½ cup dried currants
fine zest and fresh-squeezed juice of 1 orange
2 tablespoons fresh, chopped chives
2 tablespoons extra virgin olive oil
salt and freshly ground pepper to taste

Prepare CRISPY WILD RICE and toss well with the remaining ingredients.

Garden Carrots in Lemon Butter and Cumin

Serves 4

1 pound fresh-picked carrots

3 tablespoons unsalted butter

½ cup water

1 tablespoon fresh lemon juice

1 teaspoon whole cumin seeds

salt and freshly ground pepper

1 teaspoon chopped fresh Italian flatleaf parsley

1   Bring a large pot of salted water to a rapid boil. Peel the carrots and slice on the diagonal into ¼-inch-thick coins.

2   Blanch the carrots for 3 minutes. Drain in a colander and rinse in very cold water until the carrots are cool and bright orange in color.

3   Melt the butter in a large skillet over medium heat. Add the ½ cup water, lemon juice, and cumin seeds. Add the blanched carrots; cover and steam until hot. Season to taste with salt and pepper.

4   To serve, transfer to a serving dish and sprinkle with chopped fresh parsley.

Wild Mushroom
Couscous

8 ounces cepes, chanterelles, or other wild mushrooms *(substitute domestic)*

¼ cup unsalted butter

1 sprig fresh savory or rosemary

2 cups hot Chicken Stock *(see page 16)* **or use unsalted if canned**

2 tablespoons chopped fresh Italian flatleaf parsley

salt and freshly ground pepper

2 cups uncooked couscous (large-grained Israeli couscous if available)

¼ cup grated imported Gruyere cheese

1   Brush the mushrooms clean and cut into very thin slices.

2   Heat the butter in a large skillet. Add the mushrooms and the herb sprig and sauté until the liquid has evaporated and the mushrooms are lightly browned. Add the hot stock and chopped parsley. Stir and bring to a simmer. Season to taste with salt and pepper.

3   Place the uncooked couscous in a deep ceramic bowl. Pour the hot stock and mushroom mixture over the couscous. Cover tightly with plastic wrap and let stand for 10 to 15 minutes, or until all the liquid has been absorbed.

4   To serve, toss and break up the couscous grains. Adjust the seasoning and use additional butter to taste. Transfer to a warm serving dish and top with cheese.

WHOLE WHEAT BLINI
IN WALNUT OIL

SERVES 4 TO 6

Tender "pancakes"—a good wrapper for smoked game meat
or a spoonful of warm MUSHROOM DUXELLES WITH SMOKED HAM *(see page 126).*
Or simply add butter, Vermont maple syrup, and a side of black bear bacon,
widely available from game and specialty meat purveyors (see page xv).

2 cups whole wheat flour

2 eggs, separated

1 teaspoon sugar

¼ teaspoon salt

⅛-ounce cube of compressed yeast, or 2 teaspoons active dry yeast

1½ cups warm whole milk

walnut oil for frying

1   In large mixing bowl, combine 1 cup of the flour, the egg yolks, sugar, and salt. Dissolve the yeast in 1 cup of the warm milk. Add this to the flour mixture and stir well to make a soft dough. Cover the bowl loosely with a damp towel, set in a warm place, and let rise until double in volume.

2   After the dough has risen, beat in the remaining flour, then the remaining warm milk. Again cover the bowl with a damp towel and let the dough rise until doubled.

3   Beat the egg whites into stiff peaks. Stir the dough to check the consistency—it should be smooth and batterlike. If it is too stiff, add a bit more warm milk a spoonful at a time. Once the dough can be easily stirred, fold in the egg whites.

4   Lightly coat the inside of a heavy skillet with the walnut oil, then heat the pan. Drop in the batter by tablespoons and cook the blini until they are golden brown, 1 or 2 minutes on each side. They should be thin and light, about 3 inches in diameter.

Fricassee of Oyster Plant (Wild Salsify)

Serves 4

Salsify is a long, white, taproot vegetable. It is sometimes available through specialty food stores and produce merchants, vacuum-packed to preserve freshness. If you can't find it, fresh white asparagus is a good alternative.

6 tablespoons freshly squeezed lemon juice

6 cups water

1 pound fresh oyster plant, or salsify

(substitute one 10- to 12-ounce jar or can if fresh salsify is unavailable, or substitute white asparagus)

½ teaspoon salt

3 tablespoons unsalted butter

⅔ cup finely chopped onions or shallots, or a combination

½ cup finely chopped celery

1 clove minced garlic

salt and freshly ground pepper to taste

1 In a large glass mixing bowl combine 3 tablespoons of lemon juice and 3 cups of water to make "acidulated" water that will prevent the oyster plant from darkening once it is peeled. Quickly trim the roots and peel the oyster plant and drop into the water.

2 In a large saucepan or Dutch oven, add the remaining water and lemon juice. Add the ½ teaspoon of salt.

3 Remove the oyster plant, one at a time, from the acidulated water, and cut each into 3-inch-long pieces, dropping them as you go into the saucepan or Dutch oven.

4 Bring to a boil and simmer 5 to 7 minutes, until the oyster plant is tender, but still firm (taste test for doneness). Drain immediately.

5 In a sauté pan, melt the butter over medium-high heat and cook the onion (and/or shallots), celery, and garlic until golden, about 5 minutes.

6 Add the oyster plant, tossing it gently with the other ingredients until hot. Season to taste with salt and fresh pepper.

Mushroom Duxelles
with Smoked Ham

SERVES 4 AS A LIGHT SIDE DISH

*A classic duxelles of minced mushrooms is a versatile dish
that can be used to stuff poultry, fish, or omelettes. A heaping spoonful
makes a luscious accompaniment for any game meat.*

12 ounces button mushrooms
6 medium-sized shallots
4 tablespoons unsalted butter
4 ounces smoked ham, cut into fine julienne slices
salt and freshly ground pepper to taste
¼ cup Madeira
¾ cup heavy cream

1   Wipe the mushrooms clean—do not rinse or soak them in water—then mince them fine with a chef's knife. NOTE: to achieve the best result with this version of classic duxelles, do the chopping by hand. Do not use a food processor or blender. Wrap the minced mushrooms in a clean, dry kitchen towel and set aside.

2   Mince the shallots. Heat 3 tablespoons of butter in a small (2 quart) stove-top casserole or heavy skillet. Add the shallots and cook over medium-low heat, stirring constantly with a wooden spoon, until they are soft.

3   Add the remaining tablespoon of butter, the mushrooms and the ham. Cook, stirring constantly, until all the pan liquid has evaporated. Season to taste with salt and pepper.

4   To finish, add the Madeira and cream. Heat through, but do not boil. Serve as a rich accompaniment to any game dish.

Braised Belgian Endive with Chestnuts

Serves 4

An elegant autumn side dish for any kind of game.

8 ounces belgian endive
8 ounces fresh, peeled chestnuts, or canned chestnuts
1 ounce smoked bacon, chopped
salt and freshly ground black pepper
4 tablespoons of unsalted butter, soft
2 tablespoons fresh, minced parsley

1   Trim and discard the bottoms from the endive and slice the leaves into 1- to 1½-inch pieces.

2   If using fresh chestnuts: With a sharp, pointed knife, make a small slit in the flat side of each chestnut. Place them in a saucepan and cover with cold water. Bring the pan to a boil and cook the chestnuts for 1 minute.

3   Remove the chestnuts from the pan 3 or 4 at a time and carefully peel away the outer and inner skins. If the skins do not come off easily, drop the chestnuts into boiling water again for a minute or two.

4   Cook the bacon in a saucepan until it begins to brown, about 4 to 6 minutes. Add the sliced endive and chestnuts. Toss the ingredients over medium heat for about 1 minute. Add just enough water to cover, about 1½ cups. Season lightly with salt and freshly ground pepper.

5   Cover and simmer for 30 minutes if using fresh chestnuts, or 15 minutes if using canned chestnuts.

6   Drain the mixture thoroughly and place in a serving dish. Dot with soft butter and sprinkle with fresh minced parsley.

Braised
Red Cabbage

MAKES 4 SERVINGS

*A hearty accompaniment with a sweet-and-sour flavor that
will enhance any game meat or roasted pork entrée.*

1 pound red cabbage
2 tablespoons smoked bacon fat
1 medium red onion, coarsely diced
1½ cups water
1 Granny Smith apple, cored, peeled, and coarsely diced
1 ounce red wine vinegar
2 ounces honey
salt and freshly ground black pepper
3 ounces crème de cassis

1   Cut the cabbage into thin strips approximately 2 inches long and ½ wide.

2   Melt the bacon fat in a heavy saucepan over medium heat. Add the onion and cook
    for about 2 minutes. Add the cabbage and cook, stirring often, until it begins to
    soften, about 7 to 10 minutes. Add the water.

3   Add the apple, red wine vinegar, and honey. Season lightly with salt and pepper.
    Bring to a boil, then lower heat to a simmer. Cook, covered, for 20 minutes.

4   Finish by stirring in the crème de cassis and additional salt and pepper to taste.
    Serve very hot.

BED OF BRAISED ONIONS
FOR ROASTED GAME

SERVES 4

*An easy and delicious garnish for your favorite roasted game meat or fowl.
Slow cooking sweetens the onions. Make a bed of braised onions in the center
of the plate and top with slices of hot, roasted meat.*

2 pounds white onions
3 tablespoons unsalted butter
3 tablespoons olive oil
salt and freshly ground white pepper
pinch of sugar

*Optional: enrich this dish by tossing in cooked, chopped bacon and 1 or 2 teaspoons
of fresh, chopped thyme leaves in the last few moments to add a burst of flavor.*

1   Peel and chop the onions. In a large skillet, combine the butter and oil over low heat.
Add the onions and sauté them, stirring constantly, until they are very soft and
golden, but not browned, about 20 to 30 minutes.

2   Season to taste with salt and white pepper and a pinch of sugar. Serve hot.

"To eat is a necessity, but to eat intelligently is an art."
—LA ROCHEFOUCAULD

ENHANCING THE HUNTER'S TABLE
Sauces & Extras

Country Herb
and Roquefort Butter

Yields 1 cup

*Top hot grilled venison or steak with a tablespoon
of this delicious spread. Great for hot breads,
sandwiches, and baked potatoes, too.*

1 cup unsalted butter, softened
1 tablespoon minced shallots
1 tablespoon chopped fresh tarragon leaves
2 tablespoons chopped fresh Italian flatleaf parsley
2 teaspoons prepared Dijon mustard
¼ cup crumbled Roquefort cheese

1   Place all the ingredients, except for the Roquefort, in the bowl of a food processor. Pulse quickly once or twice to blend.

2   Scrape the butter mixture into a small mixing bowl and fold in the crumbled cheese. Cover tightly and store in the refrigerator or freezer until ready to use.

The Art of Breadmaking

"Either you have the hand for breadmaking, or you do not," says Chef Blondin. "Only experiment and experience will tell you if you have the hand for it."

Everything affects the results when you make bread: the ingredients, the equipment, even the weather. A humid day will make for a tough loaf. Too many restaurants boast about baking their own "house" bread, says Blondin. "But I would rather buy a good loaf from someone who has the hand for sure."

Hunter's Focaccia with Garlic and Herbs

Makes 1 Focaccia-style loaf, or 8 crusty rolls

1¾ cup warm water

1 teaspoon sugar

2½ teaspoons active dry yeast

5½ cups all-purpose flour, plus ¼ cup extra for the work surface

1 teaspoon salt

3 tablespoons olive oil

3 tablespoons oil-packed sun-dried tomatoes, drained and chopped

3 tablespoons thinly sliced white onion

1 tablespoon minced garlic

2 teaspoons chopped fresh rosemary leaves

1   In a small mixing bowl stir together the warm water, sugar, and yeast until dissolved. Cover loosely with plastic wrap or a kitchen towel and set aside for 15 minutes.

2   Using a large wooden spoon or paddle, mix in the flour, salt, and olive oil. Add the sun-dried tomatoes, onion, garlic, and rosemary, and blend into the dough thoroughly.

3   Cover again and let the dough proof in the bowl for about 40 minutes, undisturbed in a warm and draft-free place.

4   Turn the dough out onto a lightly floured work surface. Gently turn and knead the dough once or twice only. To make rolls, divide the dough into 8 equal balls and roll each gently between the work surface and the palm of your hand to smooth. Space the rolls evenly on the cookie sheet, leaving at least two inches between them. For a loaf, shape the dough into smooth ball, then push to flatten with your fingers to make a rough10-inch round of dough, similar to a pizza crust. Again, cover the dough (rolls or loaf) loosely and set aside to rise for 1 hour.

5   Preheat the oven to 400°F. Bake rolls 14 to 18 minutes until golden brown; bake a loaf slightly longer, 15 to 20 minutes.

TOMATO FONDUE

YIELDS 2 TO 3 CUPS

This chunky spread of ripe tomatoes and garlic is a versatile sauce.
Toss it with hot pasta or spread it over warm slices of fresh bread.
And it's an excellent accompaniment to chilled
GULF SHRIMP SALAD WITH PISTACHIOS *(see page 41).*

16 large Italian plum tomatoes, very ripe
(substitute two 28-ounce cans imported plum tomatoes packed in juice)
2 tablespoons extra virgin olive oil
1 large white onion, finely diced
6 cloves fresh garlic, minced
1 tablespoon chopped fresh thyme leaves
2 tablespoons unsalted butter
salt and freshly ground pepper to taste

NOTE: if using canned tomatoes, proceed to Step 3.

1   In a large stockpot bring 12 cups of water to a full boil. Prepare an ice bath by filling a large mixing bowl with cold water and ice.

2   Trim the stems from the fresh tomatoes and score a small X in the stem end of each. Blanch the tomatoes in the boiling water for 2 minutes, then drain quickly and plunge them into the ice bath.

3   Peel, halve, and seed the tomatoes over a large bowl to collect the excess juices. If using canned tomatoes, drain and seed them, removing any stems or peelings.

4   Heat the olive oil in a heavy saucepan and cook the onion and garlic over medium-low heat until translucent. Add the tomatoes, and strain in any reserved tomato juice. Add the thyme and stir.

5   Simmer for 2 hours, partially covered and stirring often, to achieve a chunky paste. Finish by adding the butter and salt and pepper to taste.

RED CURRANT SAUCE
FOR GAME

MAKES 3 CUPS

*A sweet and delicious counterpoint to the strong flavor of roasted
or grilled wild game. The cream in this recipe is optional. Chef Blondin recommends adding
cream when the sauce is served with true wild game to lend a mellow contrast to the fuller
flavor of the meat. Omit the cream when using milder flavored, farm-raised varieties. But this
is strictly a matter of personal preference, so use the cream if it suits your taste! Either way,
this sauce is a must with* MOUSSELINE OF WILD HARE *(see page 36).*

1 teaspoon cornstarch
¼ cup good-quality port wine
3 cups RICH GAME STOCK *(see page 14)*
½ cup red currant jelly
1 cup heavy cream
salt and freshly ground pepper

1   Stir the cornstarch into the Port wine until smooth.

2   Bring the stock to a boil. Whisk in the port-cornstarch mixture and the red
currant jelly.

3   Simmer for about 15 minutes to reduce the sauce, stirring frequently with a wooden
spoon until thickened. If using cream, add it at this point and reheat the sauce, but
do not boil.

4   Finish by seasoning lightly with salt and freshly ground pepper to taste. Serve with
MOUSSELINE OF WILD HARE *(see page 36)* and sweet carrots.

Port Wine
Barbecue Sauce
for Grilled Game

Makes about 2¼ cups

A spicy condiment for any grilled meat or poultry.

1 tablespoon diced shallots
zest and juice of half an orange
zest and juice of half a lemon
3 tablespoons red currant or cranberry jelly or jam
½ cup port
½ teaspoon of finely grated fresh ginger
1 tablespoon of prepared Dijon mustard
1 cup Scratch-Made Mayonnaise *(see page 51)* **or ready-made**
salt and freshly ground black pepper to taste
a large pinch cayenne pepper, or more to taste

1   Blanch the shallots in boiling water for a minute or two and drain thoroughly. Repeat with the citrus zest and set aside.

2   In a small mixing bowl, whisk together the jelly or jam, port, juices, grated ginger, and reserved shallots and citrus zest. Fold in the mustard and mayonnaise. Season with salt, pepper, and cayenne to taste. Cover and refrigerate for at least 4 hours prior to serving to allow the flavors to develop.

3   To serve, stir the sauce again and spoon into a decorative ramekin to place alongside hot grilled or broiled game.

SCRATCH-MADE TARTAR SAUCE FOR GAME FISH

MAKES 2 CUPS

*A tangy condiment for fish — but get creative and
use it on salads and sandwiches if you like!*

2 egg yolks
2 tablespoons prepared Dijon mustard
generous pinch of freshly ground black pepper
1 ¼ cup canola oil
2 tablespoons warm (not hot) red wine vinegar
3 hard-cooked eggs, finely chopped
3 tablespoons capers, drained and chopped
¼ cup minced white onions
2 tablespoons French cornichons (tiny vinegar pickles), chopped
2 tablespoons chopped fresh Italian flatleaf parsley
2 teaspoons chopped fresh chives, plus additional for garnish

1   Place the egg yolks, mustard, and pepper in the bowl of a food processor. With the motor running, slowly drizzle in the canola oil to make an emulsion, or mayonnaise.

2   Transfer the mixture to a bowl and whisk in the warm vinegar, then fold in the remaining ingredients. Add salt to taste and garnish with additional chopped chives. Chill before serving.

Fresh Green Pea Coulis

Yields 1½ cups

A splash of vivid color on the plate, this simple pea coulis makes a beautiful garnish for cold appetizers or poultry dishes. Dot or drizzle the coulis creatively around the plate for a bold presentation.

large bowl of ice water
8 cups water
½ teaspoon salt
2 cups fresh garden peas

1   Prepare a bowl of ice water. Bring 8 cups water to a full boil and add the salt.

2   Blanch the peas for 3 to 5 minutes, or until tender. Drain the peas quickly, then drop them into the ice water to cool them and to enhance their color.

3   Drain the peas very thoroughly, then transfer to the bowl of a food processor to make a fine puree. Add water by the teaspoon, if needed, to achieve a smooth sauce.

4   Strain the coulis through a fine wire mesh or chinois. Cover and refrigerate until ready to serve.

Soubise Sauce

Yields 2 cups

A buttery and mellow puree of slow-cooked onions,
Soubise Sauce *is a classic accompaniment for roasted,*
grilled, or pan-seared game, fish, or poultry.

3 large white onions, peeled and thinly sliced
6 tablespoons unsalted butter
salt and freshly ground white pepper to taste

1   Rinse the sliced onions in cold water and drain in a colander.

2   Bring a large stockpot of water (about 12 cups) to a rapid boil.

3   Plunge the onions into the boiling water and simmer for 10 minutes. Pour into a colander and drain thoroughly.

4   Melt the butter in a heavy saucepan and add the onions. Cook over very low heat (do not brown), stirring often, for about 30 minutes or until the onions are very soft.

5   Transfer the onions to the bowl of a food processor and puree. Season the sauce to taste with salt and white pepper.

RENDERED
DUCK FAT

YIELDS ABOUT 1 QUART

Duck fat has a rich flavor prized by French chefs. It is used to sauté vegetables for soup and stew, for pan-searing, and as a basting liquid for roasted game meat and poultry. A sealed container of duck fat will keep for three weeks in the refrigerator or can be kept for months in the freezer.

skin from 4 large ducks, Muscovy or mallard

Grind the skin through the fine blade of a meat grinder. Place in a large, heavy saucepan over the lowest heat setting. Render the fat from the skin for 4 to 5 hours. Strain the fat through a fine wire mesh into a clean glass jar. Let cool; seal and refrigerate.

CLASSIC
BÉCHAMEL SAUCE

YIELDS 2½ CUPS

*Use this classic béchamel creatively as the base for many casseroles
and cream sauces to enhance vegetables, fowl, or fish.*

3 tablespoons unsalted butter
3 tablespoons flour
1 cup whole milk
1 cup RICH CHICKEN STOCK *(see page 16)*
salt and freshly ground pepper to taste
pinch of grated nutmeg

1   Heat the milk but do not boil. Set aside. In a separate pan, warm the stock.

2   Melt the butter in a heavy saucepan and whisk in the flour. Cook, stirring constantly, over low heat for five minutes. Whisk in the hot milk and chicken stock and bring to a low boil. Simmer for an additional 10 minutes to thicken the sauce, whisking often. Season lightly with salt, pepper, and nutmeg.

3   Strain the sauce through a fine wire mesh or chinois.

HUNTER'S
HEARTH LIQUEUR

MAKES 3 QUARTS

Sharing a glass of this special liqueur is a tradition in rural France, where hunters guard their own secret recipes. Here is one authentic version.

1 orange
½ lemon
1¾ cups vodka
3 bottles good red wine such as Syrah or Zinfandel
2 cups sugar
½ whole vanilla bean, split open lengthwise

1　Wash the orange and lemon thoroughly, then cut the orange and the lemon into very thin slices.

2　In a large ceramic bowl, combine the vodka and the wine. Add the orange and lemon slices, the sugar, and the vanilla bean. DO NOT STIR.

3　Cover the bowl with a ceramic plate and set aside where it can rest undisturbed at room temperature for 3 weeks.

4　On the second day, and each day thereafter stir the liqueur once only for about 10 seconds with a wooden spoon and cover again with the plate.

5　After 3 weeks, strain the liqueur into a decorative bottle or decanter and chill. HUNTER'S LIQUEUR will keep, refrigerated, for about 8 months.

CHEF BLONDIN'S HUNTER'S HEARTH LIQUEUR

"Years ago, maybe during the war, you would find a bottle of this in every icebox in every farmhouse in the French countryside. It's a bit like a Spanish sangria, people tell me. A very old man from Lyon gave me this recipe a long time ago when I was first starting out as a chef. He was an old friend of the family whose name I am sorry I have forgotten."

—Richard Blondin

"MY WORST KITCHEN DISASTER?"
SAYS CHEF BLONDIN…

"I was apprenticing in the restaurant of the famous Pierre Orsi in Lyon under the direction of a chef who ranked somewhere between Orsi and myself. I was told to make ready the vanilla beans for some dessert preparation. I was carefully splitting the expensive beans down the center and removing the inner seeds—then pitching them in a garbage can! I didn't know at the time that it was the inner seed that carries the flavor. I missed the blows, but Orsi yelled—no, *screamed*—at the department chef who was my teacher. I won't forget that."

A Warm Apple Tart...

Paul Bocuse was, and is, a great traveler. He is the reigning "Pope of Chef's" as they say in France, following the lead of the most famous chefs of the last hundred years—Auguste Escoffier, Fernand Point, Antonin Carême.

Upon his return to Lyon after a long journey he looked forward to his favorite dessert—a warm apple tart seasoned with fresh rosemary. As soon as Bocuse arrived, the executive chef in charge of the restaurant would turn to the young pastry chef Richard Blondin and say, "You know what to do."

"I have discovered that there is romance in food when romance has disappeared from everywhere else."

—Ernest Hemingway

Desserts for the Hunter's Table

Warm Apple Tart with Rosemary

Makes 4 individual tarts

10 ounces frozen puff pastry
5 Golden Delicious apples
(substitute Anjou pears)
½ cup unsalted butter, divided in half
⅓ cup plus 4 tablespoons sugar
½ teaspoon fresh rosemary leaves, chopped fine
4 unblemished mint sprigs
3 tablespoons sifted powdered sugar

1   Thaw the pastry and on a floured surface, roll it out to ½-inch thickness. Cut out 4 rounds, each 5 inches in diameter. Transfer the rounds to a baking sheet lined with parchment or waxed paper and refrigerate for at least 25 minutes.

2   Peel, core, and finely dice 1 apple (or pear). Place it in a small saucepan with ⅓ cup sugar and half the butter. Cook over low heat until the apple is very soft and the sugar is dissolved to make a spreadable compote. Set the pan aside to cool.

3   Preheat the oven to 350°F. Cut four 6-inch squares of parchment or waxed paper. Arrange the squares on a baking sheet and sprinkle 2 tablespoons of sugar evenly over the sheets. Place the pastry rounds on top of the sugar and prick the entire surface of the dough with a fork.

4   Spread a tablespoon of cooled apple compote over each pastry round. Sprinkle the rosemary evenly over the compote. Peel, core, and thinly slice the remaining apples (or pears). Fan the slices out in a circular pattern on top of the tarts.

5   In a small saucepan, melt the remaining butter. With a pastry brush, coat the tops of the tarts carefully. Sprinkle the remaining 2 tablespoons of sugar over the tarts.

6   Bake for 18 minutes, or until the apples begin to caramelize, turning light golden brown. Serve hot on dessert plates, dusted with powdered sugar and garnished with a mint sprig.

Dark Chocolate Tart

Serves 6

One Pâte Sucre tart shell, prebaked *(see below)*
2 tablespoons sugar
7 tablespoons unsalted butter, very soft
5 ounces imported semisweet chocolate, such as Callebaut brand
1 whole egg
2 egg yolks

1 Prepare the tart shell and set aside. Preheat the oven to 350°F.

2 Melt the chocolate in the top of a double boiler over low heat. Set aside.

3 In mixing bowl, cream the sugar and butter together until smooth. Whisk in the whole egg, then each egg yolk, one at a time, until light and fluffy.

4 Whisk the cooled chocolate into the butter and egg mixture. Pour into the prebaked tart shell and bake for 15 minutes. Remove the tart from the oven and let cool completely, then chill before serving.

Basic Pâte Sucre Tart Shell

10 tablespoons unsalted butter, very soft
¾ cup sifted confectioner's sugar
2 eggs
1⅔ cups sifted all-purpose flour

1 Preheat oven to 350°F. In a mixing bowl cream the butter and sugar together. Mix in the eggs, then the flour.

2 Turn the dough out onto a flour-dusted work surface. Shape into a smooth, flat ball, then roll the dough to ¼-inch thickness. Transfer the dough to a 9-inch tart pan and press into the bottom and sides of the pan. Chill for 1 hour before baking.

3 Place pie weights inside the tart shell and bake for 5 to 7 minutes until light golden.

WHITE CHOCOLATE MOUSSE
WITH CHAMBORD

SERVES 6

*For this lavish dessert, use only the finest imported white chocolate available,
such as Callebaut brand from Belgium or Carma brand from Switzerland.
Chambord is a ruby-colored raspberry liqueur from France, widely available in
the U.S. Frangelico, a hazelnut liqueur, also works in this recipe, if you prefer.*

14 ounces solid white chocolate
⅔ cup half and half
1 quart heavy cream (4 cups)
¼ cup Chambord
1 tablespoon powdered unflavored gelatin
5 eggs, separated
2 tablespoons sugar
red raspberries for garnish

1 Have ready 6 decorative dessert molds or 8-ounce stemmed glasses. In the top of a
   double boiler, melt the chocolate with the half and half, stirring constantly. Set aside
   to cool slightly.

2 In a large mixing bowl, whip the heavy cream into stiff peaks and place immediately
   in the refrigerator.

3 Stir the Chambord and the gelatin powder into the chocolate mixture.

4 In a chilled mixing bowl, beat the egg whites into stiff peaks, gradually adding
   all the sugar.

5 Whisk the egg yolks into the chocolate and Chambord mixture. Gently fold the
   chocolate mixture into the whipped cream until fully incorporated, then fold in the
   beaten egg whites.

6 When the mousse is smooth and fully mixed, spoon it into the individual molds or
   glasses and chill until ready to serve. Garnish with red raspberries.

Orange Butter Cake
with Grand Marnier

¾ cup plus 1 tablespoon unsalted butter, at room temperature

3 medium juicy oranges

¾ cup granulated sugar

3 extra large whole eggs

½ teaspoon baking powder

1⅓ cups all-purpose flour

¾ cup confectioner's sugar

2 tablespoons Grand Marnier

1   Preheat the oven to 350°F. Use 1 tablespoon butter to coat an 8x8-inch square cake pan. Dust with flour.

2   Remove the dark orange peel from 2 oranges using a citrus zester or fine grater, or use a sharp paring knife, then mince the peel. *(Be careful not to include the bitter tasting white pith of the orange skin.)* Squeeze and strain the juice from the oranges and set aside.

3   Using the paddle attachment of an electric mixer on medium speed, cream the butter and granulated sugar together until light. (If mixing by hand, use a wide rubber spatula.) Mix in the eggs one at a time, then blend in the orange zest and ⅓ cup of the orange juice. Sift the flour with the baking powder, then gently fold it into the batter.

4   Turn the batter into the prepared cake pan and bake for 20 minutes, or until a toothpick inserted in the center of the cake comes out clean.

5   In a small saucepan, mix the confectioner's sugar with the remaining orange juice and the Grand Marnier. Bring just to a boil to make a light syrup. While the cake is still very warm, invert it onto a serving plate to unmold. Drizzle on the warm Grand Marnier syrup very slowly, so that it is absorbed into the cake. Serve at room temperature, or chilled, with a dollop of whipped cream, garnished with an additional pinch of zest.

Moist Walnut Butter Cake with Hot Caramel

Serves 6 to 8

Drizzle slices of this nutty cake with
Hot French Sauce Caramel *(see page 151).*
*This recipe uses walnuts, but virtually any nut can be substituted
including pecans, pistachios, or hazelnuts.*

½ cup plus 1 tablespoon unsalted butter, softened
1 cup granulated sugar
pinch of salt
5 extra large whole eggs
2 cups coarsely ground walnuts
⅔ cup sifted all-purpose flour

1   Use 1 tablespoon of soft butter to thoroughly coat the inside of a decorative 8-inch round cake mold or bundt pan. Preheat the oven to 350°F.

2   Using the paddle attachment of an electric mixer on medium speed, cream the remaining ½ cup butter with the sugar until light. (If mixing by hand, use a wide rubber spatula.) Blend in the salt, then the eggs one by one.

3   Add the flour and walnuts and stir just until the ingredients are mixed. Pour the batter into the cake mold and bake for approximately 16 to 20 minutes, until a toothpick inserted in the center of the cake comes out clean.

4   Let the cake rest for 10 minutes to cool slightly, then unmold. Arrange slices on individual dessert plates and drizzle with Hot French Sauce Caramel *(see page 151.)* Garnish with a mint sprig or a small fresh flower.

Hot French Sauce Caramel

Makes 1½ cups, enough for
one Walnut Butter Cake

1 cup granulated sugar

¼ cup water

½ cup heavy cream

½ cup chilled butter, cut into pieces

1   In a deep, heavy saucepan (see step 2), stir together the sugar and water over low heat to make a syrup. Continue to stir until the syrup begins to thicken and take on a brown, caramel color, about 15 minutes.

2   Remove the pan from the heat and slowly drizzle all the cream into the hot caramel. The cream should rise to a boil as it hits the hot syrup—use a deep saucepan so that the pot does not boil over.

3   Whisk in the butter until completely incorporated. Strain the sauce through a fine wire mesh or chinois to remove any lumps.

4   Warm the sauce when ready to use but, to maintain a smooth consistency, do not return to a boil.

Pistachio-Orange Frangipane

MAKES 2 CUPS, ENOUGH FOR ONE TART

This traditional frangipane can be used as a filling for tarts, small cakes such as petits fours, or other pastries. For a tart, begin by preparing a BASIC PÂTE SUCRE TART SHELL *(see page 147).*

6 tablespoons candied orange rind (available at specialty stores)
6 tablespoons shelled pistachios (unsalted)
¾ cup soft, unsalted butter
6 tablespoons sugar
¾ cup whole eggs, unbeaten (about 5)

1 Grind the candied orange rind and pistachios together through a food mill or food processor to make a fine meal. Set aside.

2 In a small mixing bowl cream the butter and sugar together until light and fluffy. Blend in the ground candied orange rind and pistachio mixture.

3 Using an electric mixer on low speed, beat in eggs by pouring them into the batter, one yolk at a time. Thoroughly incorporate each yolk before adding the next.

4 Pour the mixture into the tart shell and bake at 350°F for 12 to 15 minutes. Serve warm or chilled, topped with fresh berries.

BRANDIED
SOUR CHERRY CLAFOUTIS

SERVES 6

2 cups fresh sour cherries, pitted

1 cup brandy

7 tablespoons unsalted butter

7 tablespoons all-purpose flour

7 tablespoons sugar

1 tablespoon baking powder

5 extra large whole eggs

7 tablespoons whole milk

2 cups almond flour (available in specialty stores)

1   Soak the cherries in the brandy overnight.

2   Melt the butter and let cool. Set aside.

3   Preheat the oven to 350°F. Generously butter an 8-inch cake pan.

4   In a medium mixing bowl, combine the all-purpose flour, sugar, and baking powder.

5   In another bowl, whisk together the eggs and the milk. Mix into the dry ingredients to make a batter.

6   Combine the almond flour and cooled melted butter, then fold this mixture into the batter.

7   Pour the cherries, along with the brandy, into the bottom of the prepared cake pan. Spoon the clafoutis batter evenly over the cherries—it should just barely cover them.

8   Bake for 30 to 40 minutes until the top of the clafoutis is golden and the center is firm.

9   When done, invert the hot pan onto a rack to unmold the clafoutis. Let cool before slicing.

INDEX